This history is dedicated to

all members of the Orchestra

past and present

RÉAMHRÁ

Is údar ceiliúrtha de dhealramh é leathchéad bliain de cheoltóireacht leanúnach.

Nuair a bhí an chéad cheolchoirm riamh ag Ceolfhoireann Shiansach Radio Éireann, mar a tugtaí uirthi, ar an 14 Feabhra 1948, tionscnaíodh ré nua. Bheadh daoine ag súil feasta go gcloisfidís stór na saothar siansach á sheinm go rialta ag ceolfhoireann chleachtaithe, lánghairmiúil.

Lean torthaí leitheadacha an oíche chinniúnach sin. D'fhéadfai saothair mhóra shiansacha ón dara leath den chéad seo caite agus ón gcéad seo féin a chloisint i gcoirmeacha beo, don chéad uair. Bhí ceirníni gramafóin na linne sin uireasach go leor, agus ba dhul chun cinn éachtach a bhí anseo. Mealladh lucht éisteachta nua i dtreo an cheoil chlasaicigh in Éirinn.

Lena chois sin, tharla bláthú go comhuaineach i gcumadóireacht an cheoil faoi thionchar Cheolfhoireann Shiansach Radio Éireann, agus RTÉ ar ball. Faoi dheoidh d'fhéadfadh cumadóirí na hÉireann a gcuid ceoil a chloisint á sheinm ina dtír féin. Is cáiliúil iad Frederick May, Walter Beckett, Brian Boydell, Aloys Fleischmann, Seoirse Bodley, Gerard Victory, John Kinsella, John Buckley, Gerald Barry, agus tuilleadh nach iad. Chruthaigh siad scoil chumadóireachta a bhí Éireannach ó bhonn, cumadóirí áirithe ag leathnú agus ag forbairt ar na foirmeacha traidisiúnta ceoil agus cumadóirí eile ag leanúint den saiocht leathan Eorpach.

Sa tréimhse dhorcha sin a tháinig sna sála ar an dara cogadh domhanda, ní raibh dóthain ceoltóirí oilte ar fáil do cheolfhoireann shiansach. Ghlac Radio Éireann chuige scata ceoltóirí ó Lár agus Oirthear na hEorpa. Ba mhór an tairbhe don tír trí chéile na ceoltóirí seo a tháinig as traidisiúin shaibhre eile. Trí mhúinteoireacht phríobháideach, trí acadaimh agus trí choláistí ceoil, roinneadar a scileanna ar ghlúin d'fhoghlaimeoirí in Éirinn. A bhuí leis na ceoltóirí iomadúla seo a tháinig thar lear chugainn, is údar mórtais againn lion na nÉireannach atá anois inár gCeolfhoireann Shiansach Náisiúnta féin agus i gceolfhoirne siansacha ar fud an domhain.

Le leathchéad bliain tá an Cheolfhoireann Shiansach maoinithe ag RTÉ le grá don cheol siansach. Mairfidh ár ngrá isteach sa mhílaois seo chugainn agus, leis sin, athdhearbhaímid go dtógfar gach céim is gá lena chinntiú gur fearr fós a éireoidh le Ceolfhoireann Shiansach na hÉireann sna blianta romhainn.

Bob Collins
Príomh-Stiúrthóir

FOREWORD

Fifty years of continuous music-making is certainly a cause for celebration.

When the Radio Éireann Symphony Orchestra, as it was then called, gave its first concert on 14 February 1948, it opened an era when people could, as a matter of course, expect to hear the symphonic repertoire played on a regular basis by a fully professional and experienced orchestra.

The consequences of that epoch-making night were far-reaching. For the first time, the largest scale symphonic works of the latter half of the last century and of the 20th century could be heard live in concert. This marked a big improvement on the rather inadequate gramophone records of the time and it won a new audience for classical music in Ireland.

It was, too, because of the Radio Éireann and later the RTÉ Symphony Orchestra that there was a parallel flowering of musical composition. At last Irish composers could hear their music played in their own country. The roll call is illustrious: Frederick May, Walter Beckett, Brian Boydell, Aloys Fleischmann, Seoirse Bodley, Gerard Victory, John Kinsella, John Buckley, Gerald Barry and many more have produced a genuine Irish school of composition, some composers enlarging and developing on our traditional music forms, other following the wider European tradition.

In those dark days after the second world war, there were simply not enough trained musicians to make up a symphony orchestra and so Radio Éireann recruited many players from Central and Eastern Europe. These musicians from rich and different musical traditions had an enormous benefit for the country as a whole. Through private teaching and through the academies and colleges of music, they passed on their skills to a generation of Irish students. It is thanks to this influx of musicians after 1945 that we can now look with pride at the number of Irish musicians who are playing not only in the National Symphony Orchestra of Ireland but in Symphony Orchestras around the world.

For fifty years RTÉ has funded the Symphony Orchestra and carried the torch for symphonic music. We intend to carry this torch right into the next millennium and, with it, renewed commitment to take every step necessary to ensure that the National Symphony Orchestra of Ireland scales even greater heights in the years to come.

Bob Collins
Director-General

INTRODUCTION

by

Fachtna Ó Hannracháin

Is mór an onóir agus an chúis áthais dom cuireadh a fháil brollach a scríobh don leabhrán seo fé Cheolfhoireann Shiansach Náisiúnta na hÉireann.

As I took my seat in the National Concert Hall for the performance of Gustav Mahler's Symphony No 2 ('Resurrection') and watched the members of the NSOI come on the platform for the opening concert of the Orchestra's Golden Jubilee Season, my thoughts went back to those far-off days of fifty years ago when the Radio Éireann Symphony Orchestra (as it then was) was in its infancy.

Those were the days of a shortage of orchestral players, of considerable financial and administrative restrictions, of a dire lack of suitable performing venues and of many doubting Thomases. But they were also the days of those who foresaw what a great potential future lay ahead for the Symphony Orchestra under the aegis of the national broadcasting service, of those who were determined to confront and overcome obstacles, and of those in Dublin and elsewhere throughout the country who gave practical and moral support when it was most needed. Most important of all, of course, were the members of the Orchestra themselves, who could always be relied on to give of their very best, irrespective of who was the conductor, whoever the soloist and no matter how unsatisfactory and inadequate the concert venues.

Not surprisingly, there was nobody on the platform for the performance of the Mahler symphony who played in the Orchestra on 14 February 1948, when the RÉSO gave its first concert in the old Phoenix Hall. But as the performance got under way, and the glorious music of Mahler filled the National Concert Hall, I envisaged in my mind's eye all those who played as members of the Orchestra during the past fifty years assembled on the platform and receiving a prolonged standing ovation from the audience in recognition of the outstanding contribution of those dedicated musicians to the musical life of Dublin and of Ireland as a whole during the past half-century.

I consider myself fortunate to have been so deeply involved with the Orchestra from the time it was formally established in 1948 until I vacated the position of Music Director in 1961. My successors continued with the work of consolidation and development and we now have a symphony orchestra of which we can be truly proud.

I congratulate the present members of the NSOI on their many noteworthy achievements and I wish them even still greater national and international successes in the years ahead.

AUTHOR'S PREFACE

At this remove my own first memories of the Radio Éireann Orchestra are vague. I was taken to the Capitol Theatre (long since demolished) in Dublin's Prince's Street North, off O'Connell Street one Sunday afternoon. A dear aunt considered it was time my musical education took a step forward from Czerny Studies, and Handel's Messiah was obviously regarded as a good introduction to the world of choral and orchestral music. My recollections of the performance by Our Lady's Choral Society are non-existent but I do remember an usherette politely telling my aunt 'there are no pictures this afternoon, madam' and being given a rather frosty riposte for her pains.

For the record the orchestra was conducted by Dr Vincent O'Brien, who had been the first Music Director of 2RN, later Radio Éireann, and led by Terry O'Connor, a formidable figure in music broadcasting in Ireland from 1926. For me however this early baptism with Handelian waters sowed the seeds of a love affair which has lasted to this day even if it passes through the odd vicissitude from time to time.

With a number of friends I began my concert-going in earnest in my mid-teens. The range of music to which we were exposed was quite extraordinary. Not only were we grounded in the classics but there was variety and excitement in the range of contemporary music on offer. My own interest in the latter was probably encouraged by the performances of Hindemith's *Mathis der Maler, Sinfonia Serena* and *Nobilissima Visione*, Stravinsky's 'Firebird', 'Petrushka' and Symphony in Three Movements and the concertos and symphonies of Prokofiev and Shostakovich which were played on a fairly regular basis.

That so much live music was available free of charge may seem remarkable nowadays but up to the time of the National Concert Hall this was taken for granted. I, for one, have certainly benefitted from this privilege and will be eternally grateful for its availability. New friendships were forged in those teenage years in the old Phoenix Hall, and happily some of them have lasted intact.

For those of us living on the south side of the River Liffey in Dublin the move of the studio concerts to the St Francis Xavier Hall was something of a culture shock, but the lure of the RÉSO was overwhelming and the trek across town was made without demur. The orchestra's later transfer to the NCH brought a new dimension to its performances and a new perspective to its audiences. It also meant south-siders were no longer obliged to cross the river.

But what of my own personal reminiscences? There was a brief period in the Phoenix Hall days when an electronic 'A' was introduced to assist the Orchestra's tuning. A smallish boxy device, it had an 'on-off' button which Renzo Marchionni pressed with his accustomed refinement. Before long, however, it was agreed that human resources could not be surpassed, and Albert Solivérès resumed his official role.

Some concerts remain in the memory, not least Isaac Stern's Beethoven Violin Concerto at the Theatre Royal; a performance of Beethoven's Triple Concerto in the Metropolitan Hall with Renzo Marchionni, Maurice Meulien and Anthony Hughes which formed a lasting fascination for me of this unusual work; the occasion of the first Irish performance of the Tippett Piano Concerto at the RDS when, after the first movement, a member of the audience emitted an audible sigh of relief; a Barbirolli Verdi *Requiem* at the National Stadium for which I was also privileged to attend some of the rehearsals; the Messiaen *Turangalîla-symphonie* at the St Francis Xavier Hall; Kyung Wha Chung playing the Berg Concerto at St Patrick's Training College, Drumcondra; Prokofiev's *The Gambler* and Janáček's *Kata Kabanova* at Wexford; the premiere of Gerard Victory's *Ultima Rerum* and John Buckley's Organ Concerto at the NCH. But these are mere drops in an ocean of memorable occasions.

While it is invidious to mention names, offence cannot be given through that of the late Audrey Park, a remarkable leader who, besides her innate musicianship, invariably brought a sense of occasion to her every appearance. There was nothing mundane about Audrey. Her marriage to Archie Collins also had a uniqueness about it, as they spent almost their entire working lives together. Jack Leydier was another charming character both on and off the concert platform. A musician through and through, he led the second violin section for many years until, like Audrey and Archie, an untimely death removed him from us. But these are only three of the myriad of artists who have given me, and many others, so much pleasure over the years.

Throughout its history the orchestra's broadcasts have been in the very capable hands of various engineers and producers. They were the unseen heroes of resolving many a technical hitch, and among those who served many years hidden away from the public eye are the now retired Éamon Timoney (father of violinist Thérèse), Jim McHale and Marcus McDonald. Anton Timoney has continued in his father's (Éamon) footsteps and has been joined by Aodhán Ó Dúill. On the production side Dennis Suttill laboured long until his retirement, while Celia Donoghue, Séamus Crimmins, Jerome de Bromhead and John Hughes continued in this important role. Through them and others, radio listeners have enjoyed a highly acceptable quality of transmission.

Fifty years have been completed and, while it is not my task to look into the future, I wish the Orchestra well *Ad multos annos* and thank each of its members past and present for the pleasure they have given me and many thousands of others over a very long period. I hope the next fifty years will be equally fruitful, that audiences will continue to be found and that they too will be as enchanted by the National Symphony Orchestra. The fact that a designated Arts and Music wavelength will be coming on stream from RTÉ in 1999 can only be good news. The assured commitment which Bob Collins, RTÉ Director-General, gave to the NSO and the Station's other performing groups when announcing plans for the 1997/98 season must also stand in good stead for the future of the musicians and of music in Ireland.

Acknowledgments

Firstly my sincere thanks to RTÉ's Music Department, through the ubiquitous Laurie Cearr, for inviting me to undertake this history. Then to Lenni McCullagh of the RTÉ Illustrations Library and Brian Lynch of RTÉ's Written Archives section for their enormous help and tolerance; to Kevin Roche, who painstakingly cast an eagle eye over the proofs; to Richard Pine for his perceptive editorial skills; and to the many others who so generously gave me their precious time and assistance - Michael Bowles, Paddy Brennan, Maureen Donohoe, Philip Gavin, Máire Larchet, Frank Murphy, Fachtna Ó hAnnracháin, Elizabeth and Oliver O'Brien, Patricia and Eimear Ó Broin, Brian O'Rourke, Colman Pearce, Hartmut (Teddy) Pritzel, Kasper de Roo, the late Albert Rosen, Simon Taylor, Air Consult International, The Music Association of Ireland, Staff of the Gilbert Library, Staff of RTÉ's Library, and the National Symphony Orchestra, without which the exercise could not have happened. I am deeply indebted to all of them.

The programmes featured opposite the text are intended as an indication of the range of programming and artists presented by the Orchestra since the 1940s, and should not be regarded as a comprehensive record of concert-giving.

Every care has been taken by the author and publishers to ensure that all details are correct, but, as some records have failed to come to light, it has not been possible to verify every programme or personal detail.

Illustrations by Philippa Bayliss.

1

BROADCASTING AND ITS ORCHESTRAS
1926-1947

From little acorns

On 14 February 1998 Ireland's music lovers celebrate the fiftieth birthday of what is today the National Symphony Orchestra. In February 1948 the Radio Éireann Symphony Orchestra was officially named, having grown from the original 'Clery's Instrumental Trio' in January 1926. Kevin Roche, a former Assistant Director of Music, now retired from Radio Telefís Éireann, put it succinctly in a radio talk he gave in 1995 when he quoted the eighteenth-century poet David Everett: 'Large streams from little fountains flow, Tall oaks from little acorns grow'.

Quite soon after its inauguration 2RN (as the Dublin Broadcasting Station was known from its call-sign) established a Station Trio. This was the renamed Clery's Instrumental Trio (so called because the same artists had played in the restaurant of Clery's department store in Dublin's O'Connell Street). Within a couple of months it had been increased by one and consisted of Terry O'Connor (violin), Rosalind Dowse (viola), Viola O'Connor (cello), who was Terry's sister, and Kitty O'Doherty (piano). By June 1926 it had become the Station Orchestra and numbered seven through the addition of Maud Aiken and Moira Flusk (violins) and Zack Lee (double-bass). Broadcasts were of course live.

On 26 November 1927 Vincent O'Brien, undeterred by the size of his forces, even if suitably augmented for the occasion, ambitiously decided to mount a public symphony concert under the auspices of 2RN in the Metropolitan Hall in Dublin's Lower Abbey Street. He programmed Weber's *Euryanthe* Overture, Beethoven's First Symphony, the *Danse Macabre* by Saint-Saëns and the Rossini/Respighi *La Boutique Fantasque.*

In between, bass Glyn Eastmann sang Bellini's *'Vi ravviso' (La Sonnambula)* and Mozart's *'Deh, vieni alla finestra' (Don Giovanni),* Arthur Darley (violin) played Carolan's Concerto and a number of traditional Irish airs and Séamus Clandillon, who was 2RN's first Director of Broadcasting, sang several songs in Irish. The Civil Service Choir also took part and there was audience participation in the 'Adeste Fideles' and 'Let Erin Remember' among other items. It was plainly something of a marathon affair.

In the *Irish Times* review of 28 November 1927 'Obligato' explained the concert 'was declared in advance to be an experiment' but commented favourably that the Beethoven was 'clean and crisp' and the Weber 'made to sparkle freshly'.

Original 2RN Orchestra

First outside broadcast by 2RN Orchestra
(late 1920s).
(l-r): Vincent O'Brien, Kitty O'Doherty,
P.J. Duffy (organiser), Terry O'Connor,
Moira Flusk, Dina Copeman (piano soloist),
Maude Aiken, Rosalind Dowse,
Viola O'Connor, Zach Lee.

He continued:

> *In big ensemble passages a greater weight of string tone would have been desired but the wind instruments [were] so nicely managed by players from the Army School of Music that orchestral balance was seldom wanting. The quality of playing in all departments was excellent and we have an orchestra that is worthy of high praise.*
>
> *Miss Terry O'Connor, besides giving a good lead through the music as a whole, was prominent not only in the weird solo part in the Danse Macabre but also in the pizzicato accompaniment to 'Deh, vieni', which she managed with notable skill.*
>
> *The treatment of Saint-Saëns's grim joke was in accord with the evening's general insouciance and the rhythm and colour of Rossini's music were so given as to bring the ballet before our eyes.*
>
> *Towards the end of the evening Mr Clandillon spoke as if further concerts of this kind are assured, and it may be hoped so. There is a place for such evenings, not only from the Free State Broadcasting programmes, but in the musical life of Dublin's fair city.*

It may be interesting to point out that the Hallé Orchestra, under Hamilton Harty, had given two concerts (3.30pm and 6pm) at the RDS on 31 October 1927 - Beethoven's Fourth Symphony and Harty's own 'Irish Symphony' were the main works - and the recital series for RDS Members during the 1927/28 season included Walter Gieseking, Andrés Segovia, Isolde Menges, Jan Smeterlin and Alexander Brailowsky as well as various visiting and local chamber music ensembles. Concerts were also given by the Dublin Philharmonic Society and the Dublin Orchestral Society (conducted by JF Larchet and Michele Esposito) during this period.

But from where did Vincent O'Brien get his extra musicians? At the time Dublin was plentifully supplied with orchestral players who were engaged in the numerous theatres and cinemas. Many of the wind and brass players came from the Army Bands and Army School of Music which were then under the direction of Colonel Fritz Brase and his assistant Commandant Friedrich Christian Sauerzweig. Their instruments were tuned to orchestral pitch.

(In fact, until the establishment of the RÉSO in 1948, it had been common practice for all large-scale orchestral activity in Dublin to combine string players from an academic background with wind and brass players, originally from the bands of British regiments stationed in the city and, after independence, from the Free State Army.)

The result was only partly successful but more from a commercial than a musical standpoint. The audience was fairly small although the admission charge of 1s.3d [slightly over 6p, equivalent to £1.20 today], including tax, was reasonable. The concert was relayed directly by 2RN.

Attempts at similar ventures continued until 1929 when the public concerts were temporarily suspended. In the interval there had been an Homage to Schubert in part of a programme with the 2RN Symphony Orchestra and Jean Nolan (soprano) in the Metropolitan Hall on 29 January 1928. In the second half of this concert Terry O'Connor was the soloist in

Vincent O'Brien

Terry O'Connor (seated) with her successor as Leader, **Nancie Lord**

the Saint-Saëns 'Introduction and Rondo capriccioso'. On 10 April another substantial programme, conducted by Vincent O'Brien, included Beethoven's Eighth Symphony, Rimsky-Korsakov's 'Sheherazade' and a selection from Sullivan's *The Tempest* interspersed by various items from soprano Chrissie Mooney, Jean du Chastain (the Belgian piano virtuoso who briefly succeeded Esposito as Professor of Piano at the RIAM) and the Civil Service Choir under Hubert Rooney (a former pupil of Jean de Reszke who became the teacher of Veronica Dunne and an expert on plainchant).

Vincent O'Brien, who also introduced Elgar's *The Dream of Gerontius* to Ireland, conducted a number of studio opera performances at this time. On 8 January 1928 there was Donizetti's *The Daughter of the Regiment* with Joan Burke, JC Browner and William J Lemass in the cast. The following year had Offenbach's *The Tales of Hoffmann* with Joan Burke and JC Browner on 12 May; Balfe's *The Rose of Castile* with Joan Burke and William J Lemass on 31 May and Mozart's *The Marriage of Figaro,* again with Joan Burke and JC Browner among the cast on 22 June 1929. Later that year, on 12 October, there was *Il trovatore* with Edna Rees (Leonora), JC Browner and William Lemass while a concert on 12 December conducted by Vincent O'Brien had the 2RN Symphony Orchestra assisted by members of the Army No 1 Band. Harty's 'Irish Symphony'was followed by Respighi's 'The Fountains of Rome' and Tchaikovsky's '1812' Overture.

By 1933 the Station Orchestra's strength had risen to nineteen and two years later its complement was twenty-four. Interestingly both Terry O'Connor and Kitty O'Doherty married and withstood attempts to obtain their resignations as would have been obligatory under civil service rules. Terry became Mrs David Glasgow but retained her maiden 'stage' name. Kitty continued with her maiden name until she resigned from Radio Éireann in 1939. Later she used her married name of O'Callaghan and indeed more often than not was addressed as 'Mrs O'Callaghan'.

During 1933 the Irish National Music League (Dublin Branch), one of whose aims was to 'promote good music at popular prices', organised a number of Orchestral and Vocal Concerts at the Mansion House. The programme for 7 February had the 2RN Orchestra under Vincent O'Brien with soloist Douglas ffrench-Mullen in Mozart's A major Piano Concerto. Among other pieces the Orchestra played Tchaikovsky's Nutcracker Suite, a Suite for Strings by Lindsay Seymour and Percy Grainger's 'Molly on the Shore'. The orchestral items were interspersed with piano solos and two groups of songs sung by Kitty Fagan accompanied by Kitty O'Doherty. The admission charge was sixpence [2½p, or 50p today] and the programme priced at twopence.

When 2RN became Radio Éireann in 1937, its Orchestra had grown to twenty-eight musicians but its public appearances were few and far between although its broadcast performances were many and varied. Conductors were mostly visiting artists but also included the Irish musicians JM [James Michael] Doyle, Arthur Duff and Dermot O'Hara, Lieutenants in the Army School of Music,

J M Doyle

Sir Herbert Hamilton Harty

and Cork's Aloys Fleischmann. Lieut (later Colonel) Doyle, who died in 1997 aged 91, was the first Irish-born Director of the Army School of Music. He was actually seconded to the Orchestra for a year from July 1936 and again from December 1938 for a further two years after which he was recalled to the Army. Kerry-born Lieut O'Hara, who filled the gap between 1937 and 1938, returned to Radio Éireann in 1948, becoming conductor of the station's Light Orchestra the following year.

In late 1937 the policy of public concerts was revived and four concerts were given in each of the 1937/38 and 1938/39 seasons at the Gaiety Theatre in South King Street but with only a modest attendance overall. The 1937/38 conductors and soloists were Frank Bridge with Angus Morrison (piano) and George Walsh (described as Irish Basso); Constant Lambert with Vera Canning (cello) and Cecily Kenny (mezzo); Eak Tai Ahn with Maurice Cole (piano) and Hubert Valentine (tenor) and Aloys Fleischmann with Charles Lynch (piano) and Heddle Nash (tenor).

Fleischmann's programme included Frederick May's 'Spring Nocturne', his own 'Three songs for tenor and orchestra', EJ Moeran's Second Rhapsody, Ina Boyle's 'Colin Clout' of 1921 and Elizabeth Maconchy's Piano Concertino which had been premiered in Prague in 1930. Eak Tai Ahn included his own fantasia 'Korea' - a work banned in his native country. The rest of this programme was mainly Mozart arias and the C Minor K 491 Piano Concerto. Tickets ranged from one shilling to three shillings and sixpence. In November 1937 the Orchestra, 'through the courtesy of Dr TJ Kiernan' (then Director of Broadcasting), was involved with the Dublin Operatic Society at the Gaiety in performances of *La Bohème* and *Carmen* under Vincent O'Brien.

Bruckner's Fourth Symphony had a performance under Arthur Hammond on 22 September 1938 while Walton O'Donnell of BBC Northern Ireland conducted the Orchestra in Sibelius's First Symphony at the Gaiety on 23 October. The soloist in Beethoven's Third Piano Concerto was Walter Rummel. Studio concerts in November that year were conducted by Vincent O'Brien, Dermot O'Hara and Fritz Brase with E Godfrey Brown, former Musical Director of BBC Northern Ireland, conducting on 16 December.

The distinguished conductor of the French National Orchestra, Manuel Rosenthal, brought the harpist Lily Laskine to the Gaiety with Gabriel Pierné's *Concertstück* on 22 January 1939. The Orchestra visited the National Stadium on St Patrick's Day when JM Doyle conducted a programme of Irish music. Hamilton Harty conducted a number of his own works on 15 May including some of the songs with Parry Jones, and returned again on 15 October with the eminent Solomon as soloist in Tchaikovsky's First Piano Concerto. Harty's symphony in the Gaiety that evening was Brahms's Second. Applause after the first movement of the Concerto initiated letters, for and against the idea, to *The Irish Times.*

Michael Bowles conducts at the Capitol Theatre

Besides his Dublin appearances during the war years Bowles also conducted a number of concerts with the BBC Symphony Orchestra in both Bedford and London. In one of these Clifford Curzon was the soloist in Beethoven's 'Emperor' Concerto, Sibelius's First Symphony being the other main work. Another BBC programme included Dvořák's Carnival Overture, Harty's With the Wild Geese and his own Divertimento. He also conducted the BBC Northern Ireland Orchestra in Belfast on a number of occasions and the BBC Scottish Orchestra in Glasgow

In 1950, through the influence of Sir Adrian Boult, Bowles was offered the post of Conductor of the New Zealand Symphony Orchestra on a three year contract at a salary of £1,650 per annum. He did undertake two Dublin concerts ; 20 January (Beethoven's 'Pastoral' Symphony and Strauss's Till Eulenspiegel) and 28 March 1950 (Roussel's Rhapsodie Flamande and Tchaikovsky's Fourth Symphony) after which he had an 'enthusiastic and sustained ovation from both the audience and musicians'.

Returning from New Zealand, Michael Bowles conducted a number of concerts in Dublin in March and April 1954 before moving to a professorship in Indiana University and conductorship of the Indianapolis Philharmonic Society. His programmes included Debussy's First Clarinet Rhapsody with Michele Incenzo and La Mer on 2 April and Falla's Nights in the Gardens of Spain with Kitty O'Callaghan and John Gardiner's Symphony in D minor on 9 April. This concert was attended by PJ Little TD who was then also Chairman of the Arts Council.

There was another concert with the RÉSO in the Abbey Lecture Hall on 2 September 1955 which included the first performance of an American work - Bernhard Heiden's Second Symphony - but only two more since then. These took place in the Gaiety and Cork's City Hall on 16 and 17 January 1977. Bowles presented the same programme in each centre ; Moeran's Sinfonietta, Brahms's Fourth Symphony and Rachmaninov's Paganini Rhapsody with John O'Conor as soloist. This was the same piece which Charles Lynch played in the first Bowles concert in the Mansion House on 16 October 1941.

Michael Bowles as Conductor

Wartime, or 'The Emergency' as it became conventionally termed in Ireland, brought a change in musical fortunes with an upsurge in appreciation and an ever increasing number of concertgoers. While there were a number of factors involved the input of a single figure, Lieutenant, later Captain, Michael Bowles, was particularly distinctive and the importance of his contribution to Ireland's music scene in the 1940s must be stressed.

Born in Riverstown, County Sligo in 1909, Bowles joined Radio Éireann on 1 January 1941 as Conductor of its Orchestra. He found the musicians somewhat demoralised. Their terms of employment were part-time and non-pensionable. As Michael Bowles remembers, salaries were £5 per week with the leader receiving £7.

Indeed an advertisement in the daily press of 20 December 1939 read:-

Roinn Puist agus Telegrafa
BROADCASTING SERVICE

Applications are invited for the position of Trombone Player in the Irish Radio Orchestra. Pay will be at the rate of £5 a week (inclusive). The hours of attendance will be 24 a week inclusive of rehearsals.

The selected applicant will be engaged for an initial period not exceeding one year, but the engagement may be terminated sooner by one week's notice given in writing by either party to the other.

Applications in writing, stating qualifications, should be forwarded not later than the 1st January 1940 to the Secretary (Establishment Branch - Orchestra) Room 208, Department of Posts and Telegraphs, GPO, Dublin.

The musicians had five morning rehearsals and often five evening broadcasts from an unsuitable, low ceilinged studio in part of the GPO building in Dublin's Henry Street. They would be on call too at week-ends as programming needs occasionally demanded. Feedback from the listening public was virtually nil and indeed the quality of reception in many areas of the country was poor.

Bowles believed it was essential for the Orchestra to play in public, as the ability to communicate directly with a live audience was surely part and parcel of the musician's function. Firstly, however, he proposed to the Director of Broadcasting, TJ Kiernan, that the Orchestra move to a larger studio. Bowles's powers of persuasion were sufficient to get Kiernan's approval and a series of concerts were broadcast from The Scots Church Hall in nearby Lower Abbey Street. Admittedly small, the building was a vast improvement on the Henry Street premises. It also allowed an audience of about forty to attend and it gave the Orchestra a feeling of release from confinement.

Buoyed up by this modest success, Bowles became more ambitious and suggested a series of fortnightly public concerts in the Round Room of Dublin's Mansion House in Dawson Street. This too found favour and the Thursday concerts which began there in the autumn of 1941 established the precedent for many subsequent similar ventures leading to the now regular weekly concerts by the NSO at the National

30 October 1941
Mansion House

Berlioz:	Overture, 'Benvenuto Cellini'
Duff:	Suite for Strings
Saint-Saëns:	Cello Concerto
Bizet:	Symphony in C*
Wagner:	Overture, 'Die Meistersinger'

Clyde Twelvetrees, cello
Michael Bowles, conductor
**First Irish performance*

11 December 1941
Mansion House

Gomez:	Overture, 'Il Guarany'
Larchet:	Three songs
Dvořák:	Symphony no 7
Ippolitov-Ivanov:	Caucasian Sketches
Harty:	The Children of Lir
Berlioz:	Symphonie fantastique

May Devitt, soprano
Michael Bowles, conductor

15 October 1942
Mansion House

Grétry:	Ballet suite from 'Cephale e Procris'
Beethoven:	Piano Concerto no 5 ('Emperor')
Dvořák:	Symphony no 9
Chopin:	Ballade no 2
Smetana:	Bohemian caprice

Rhoda Coghill, piano
Michael Bowles, conductor

26 November 1942
Mansion House

Rossini:	Overture, 'L'Italiana in Algeri'
Brahms:	Symphony no 4
Elgar:	Enigma Variations
Tchaikovsky:	Rococo Variations
Wagner:	Overture to 'Tannhäuser'

Clyde Twelvetrees, cello
Michael Bowles, conductor

10 December 1942
Mansion House

Beethoven:	Overture, Leonora no 3
Beethoven:	Symphony no 1
Beethoven:	Violin Concerto
Harty:	With the Wild Geese

Isidore Shlaen, violin
Michael Bowles, conductor

28 January 1943
Mansion House

Gluck/Mottl:	Ballet Suite
Rubbra:	Improvisations on a Virginal Theme
Mozart:	Piano Concerto in B flat, K450
Vaughan Williams:	London Symphony
Vaughan Williams:	Overture, 'The Wasps'

Claude Biggs, piano
Michael Bowles, conductor

Concert Hall. The Board of Works was brought in to erect a stage extension which could be easily put in place before a concert and removed again the following morning. The first concert on 16 October had the renowned Cork-born Charles Lynch (who had been a pupil of York Bowen and Egon Petri) as soloist in the first Irish performance of Rachmaninov's Paganini Rhapsody. The main work was Beethoven's 'Eroica' Symphony with Mozart's *Don Giovanni* Overture, Two Irish Airs by Carl Hardebeck and Tchaikovsky's Italian Caprice completing the programme.

The attendance included the Ministers for Agriculture, Education, Justice and Posts & Telegraphs. Also present were the Belgian, French, German, and Spanish Ministers, with the Canadian High Commissioner and the British Representative. The Consuls of Japan and Sweden, the Polish Consul-General and the Swiss Chargé d'affaires also attended, as did the Lord Mayor of Dublin and the Irish international soprano Margaret Burke Sheridan.

Two points may be noted about this concert - its contemporary content (the Rachmaninov Rhapsody was composed in 1934) and the inclusion of a work by an Irish composer. The commitment of Radio Éireann, and later RTÉ, to music of the time and to the work of native composers would be on-going. With the introduction of the 'Prom' concerts in 1953 it became the Music Department's policy to programme an Irish work in each public concert, in addition to the considerable amount of music by Irish and other contemporary composers scheduled in the regular 'invitation' studio concerts and broadcasts. That this plan would be revised in the 1980s and 1990s stemmed, to a degree, from the need to be more cautious about box-office appeal in programme planning.

To the astonishment of the authorities, the concerts played to packed houses (Mansion House capacity was 750/800). *The Irish Times* reported after the first concert that *....it played to a "full house" and in every way the concert seemed to be a complete success, which augurs well for the possibility of a regular season of symphony concerts.* Such indeed was the case and public interest led to tickets being 'rationed' to four per person. Prices ranged from 1s.6d to 2s.6d.

Naturally for the public concerts, and some studio broadcasts, it was necessary to increase the strength of the Orchestra and this Bowles did by bringing in musicians from the Army to bolster the woodwind and brass. There were other excellent free-lance musicians available in Dublin - Jack Cheatle, who joined the Orchestra from the Theatre Royal in 1943 and became leader of the Radio Éireann Light Orchestra in 1948, among them - besides some ex-members of the Dublin cinema orchestras, the Philharmonic Society and teachers who supplemented the strings. Contracts were offered on an individual concert basis, with four rehearsals, but the offer of the series of engagements was an attractive incentive.

Concerts at the Capitol Theatre

Quite soon the popularity of the programmes with the public necessitated a larger venue. The Capitol Theatre, originally built as an opera house ('La Scala') but by then acting as a cinema,

20 February 1944
Capitol Theatre

Bax: Overture to a Picaresque Comedy
Fleischmann: The Humours of Carolan
Beethoven: Piano Concerto no 4
Sibelius: The Swan of Tuonela
Beethoven: Symphony no 8

Irene Scharrer, piano
Michael Bowles, conductor

5 March 1944
Capitol Theatre

Borodin: Overture to 'Prince Igor'
Prokofiev: Symphony no 1 ('Classical')
Moeran: Violin Concerto
Dvořák: Symphony no 7

Nancy Lord, violin
Michael Bowles, conductor

10 December 1944
Capitol Theatre

Dvořák: Slavonic Rhapsody no 3
Ravel: Le Tombeau de Couperin
Saint-Saëns: Piano Concerto no 2
Brahms: Symphony no 4

Moura Lympany, piano
Michael Bowles, conductor

14 January 1945
Capitol Theatre

Smetana: Overture, 'The Bartered Bride'
Hardebeck: 'Seoithín Seó'
Beethoven: Symphony no 7
Schumann: Piano Concerto
Sibelius: En Saga

Rhoda Coghill, piano
Michael Bowles, conductor

28 January 1945
Capitol Theatre

Weber: Overture, 'Der Freischütz'
Harty: John Field Suite
Mozart: Symphony no 36, K425
Bruch: Violin Concerto no 1
Bizet: Jeux d'Enfants

Marie Wilson, violin
Michael Bowles, conductor

14 October 1945
Capitol Theatre

Massenet: Overture, 'Phèdre'
Debussy: Petite Suite
Beethoven: Piano Concerto no 4
Sibelius: Symphony no 4

Jeanne-Marie Darré, piano
Michael Bowles, conductor

28 October 1945
Capitol Theatre

Mozart: Overture, 'Don Giovanni'
Mozart: Violin Concerto in D, K218
Mozart: Symphony no 35, K385
Mozart: Clarinet Concerto, K622
Elgar: 'Wand of Youth', Suite no 2
Stanford: Irish Rhapsody no 1

Arthur Franks, violin
Pat Ryan, clarinet
Michael Bowles, conductor

11 November 1945
Capitol Theatre

Bach: Brandenburg Concerto no 1
Wagner: Siegfried Idyll
Dvořák: Violin Concerto
Sibelius: Symphony no 7
Walton O'Donnell: Songs of the Gael

Max Rostal, violin
Michael Bowles, conductor

was hired to Radio Éireann on Sunday afternoons and the Orchestra's public concerts were switched from the Mansion House in the autumn of 1943. Charles Lynch, who was to become a regular and central figure in the concert schedules, played Tchaikovsky's B flat Minor Concerto in the first Capitol concert on 17 October and the theatre continued as a venue until early 1948.

The concert on 31 October 1943 (mainly Beethoven's Fifth Symphony and Rimsky-Korsakov's Sheherazade) opened with Wagner's *Rienzi* Overture and brought the following comment from *The Irish Times* next day:

> *After yesterday's experience at the Radio Éireann Symphony Concert in the Capitol Theatre those in charge should refuse admission to the auditorium the moment the conductor takes his stand on the rostrum.*
>
> *Yesterday, Captain Michael Bowles, the conductor had the unhappy experience of having to hold up his players for some minutes while late-comers pushed their way to seats with the result that the opening of the Rienzi Overture went awry. The unfortunate first trumpeter, who had a trying solo lead, became completely unnerved and had to leave the stage. Luckily the third trumpeter came to the rescue and the work proceeded and, in the circumstances, was very well played.*

Some of the soloists came from England aided and abetted most ably by a number of Irish performers, pianists Rhoda Coghill (who had been a pupil of Arthur Schnabel in Berlin and is also a composer and poet), Kitty O'Callaghan and Charles Lynch, violinists Terry O'Connor and Nancie Lord (who premiered Moeran's Concerto on 5 March 1944), with singers Renée Flynn, Kathleen Uhlemann, James Johnston and William Watt among them. Isidore Shlaen could be added to this list as he had been accepted into the Orchestra after arriving in Dublin as a refugee. The Dublin Oratorio Society invariably provided the forces for large choral works such as Beethoven's Ninth Symphony - a performance on 21 May 1944 had Renée Flynn, Kathleen Uhlemann, Robert McCullagh and Frank Cowle.

The visiting players included violinists Jelly d'Aranyi, who by all accounts gave a stunning performance of the Beethoven Concerto on 12 December 1943; Marie Wilson, deputy leader of the BBC Symphony, who played the Bruch G minor Concerto on 28 January 1945; Henry Holst, former leader of the Berlin Philharmonic, who played the Brahms Concerto on 25 February that year and Pat Ryan, the Kerry-born principal clarinet of the Hallé. As an interesting aside d'Aranyi, the evening after her Capitol concert, gave a recital for two hundred residents of the Legion of Mary's Morning Star Hostel. Accompanied by Kitty O'Callaghan, her programme was introduced by Michael Bowles.

Among pianists were Harriet Cohen, Renée Collinson (who was heard in the Dvořák Concerto in November 1944), Moura Lympany (who played the Saint-Saëns Second the following month) and Irene Scharrer in Beethoven's Fourth on 20 February 1944. The cellist Beatrice Harrison played the Elgar Concerto on 15 October 1943 while baritone Dennis Noble was on the schedule of visiting singers.

25 November 1945
Capitol Theatre

Mendelssohn:	Overture, 'A Midsummer Night's Dream'
Franck:	Symphony in D minor
Moeran:	Cello Concerto*
Handel:	Entry of the Queen of Sheba
Berlioz:	Serenade from 'Harold in Italy'
Richard Strauss:	Waltzes from 'Der Rosenkavalier'

Peers Coetmore, cello
Michael Bowles, conductor
**First Irish Performance*

9 December 1945
Capitol Theatre

Reger:	Festival Overture
Dvořák:	Serenade for strings
Rachmaninov:	Piano Concerto no 3
Beethoven:	Symphony no 3 ('Eroica')

Charles Lynch, piano
Michael Bowles, conductor

10 February 1946
Capitol Theatre

Tchaikovsky:	Italian Caprice
Dvořák:	Cello Concerto
Beethoven:	Symphony no 5

Gethyn Wykeham George, cello
Michael Bowles, conductor

13 October 1946
Capitol Theatre

Haydn:	Symphony no 101 ('Clock')
Schumann:	Piano Concerto
Sibelius:	Symphony no 5

Monique Haas, piano
Michael Bowles, conductor

27 October 1946
Capitol Theatre

Wagner:	Overture, 'The Flying Dutchman'
Wagner:	Suite from 'Die Meistersinger'
Wagner:	Liebestod from 'Tristan und Isolde'
Beethoven:	Symphony no 6 ('Pastoral')

Oda Slobodskaya, soprano
Michael Bowles, conductor

12 January 1947
Capitol Theatre

Sibelius:	En Saga
Sibelius:	Violin Concerto
Elgar:	Enigma Variations
Haydn:	Symphony no 96 ('Miracle')

Henry Holst, violin
Michael Bowles, conductor

26 January 1947
Capitol Theatre

Fleischmann:	Overture, 'The Four Masters'
Tchaikovsky:	Suite no 3
Pergolesi/ Barbirolli:	Oboe Concerto
Richard Strauss:	Oboe Concerto
Mozart:	Symphony no 30, K202

Léon Goossens, oboe
Michael Bowles, conductor

9 February 1947
Capitol Theatre

Gunnar de Frumerie:	Pastoral Suite for Flute and Strings
Wirén:	Symphony no 3
Handel:	Aria from 'Julius Caesar'
Mozart:	'O Maiden Fair and Slender' from 'The Magic Flute'
Tchaikovsky:	Finale from 'Eugene Onegin'
Tchaikovsky:	'Nutcracker' Suite

Dennis Noble, baritone
Michael Bowles, conductor

The capacity of the Capitol was more than double that of the Mansion House but again 'Full House' signs were, more often than not, the order of the day. In 1942 the ever enthusiastic Bowles managed to convince the authorities of the need to further increase the full-time strength of the Orchestra to forty, and also negotiated a small increase in pay for the musicians.

Minister PJ Little agreed that salaries should rise to £6 for the men and £5 for the ladies. This took some time to finalise, and, to circumnavigate the wartime Wages Standstill Order, the musicians' hours were raised from twenty-four to thirty per week. The positions however were still non-pensionable. Among the artists appointed was the horn player Frank Murphy, the first non-army musician in the Orchestra's brass sections, and he was soon followed by another civilian horn player, Liam McGuinness. (Both moved to the Radio Éireann Light Orchestra on its formation in 1948 and indeed some forty years later Frank Murphy would find himself seconded to the National Concert Hall as its Manager.)

But in November 1943 when moving the Estimate in Dáil Éireann the Minister, PJ Little, explained that the additional cost of the Radio Éireann Orchestra - £6,725 [£114,000 in today's money]- was mainly responsible for the increase of £8,773 in the Estimate of £78,880 for broadcasting services. Artists fees and the establishment of a choir had accounted for £2,388 [today, approximately £40,500].

In the same debate Deputy J McCann referring to the Department's 'parsimonious' policy to Radio Éireann, said it had been left little better than an amateur concert hall. The Minister had given them a first-rate orchestra - although he was sorry it was not composed completely of Irish nationals - but would £5 pay for a first-rate male performer or £4 for a lady?

Michael Bowles as Director of Music

Vincent O'Brien resigned as Radio Éireann's Director of Music in April 1941 and Michael Bowles, who became Acting Director in 1942, was appointed officially as Director of Music, by the Civil Service Commission and on the insistence of the Director of Broadcasting, PJ Kiernan, from December 1944. Holding the post in conjunction with his job as Conductor of the Radio Éireann Orchestra, he resigned from the Army. His staff consisted of a Grade I typist and a Grade III clerical assistant. With Bowles they looked after the administrative side of the Orchestra, as well as taking care of all the arrangements involved with the public concerts.

Arthur Duff, who had been Studio Control Officer and Balance and Control Officer, was appointed Assistant Music Director in October 1945. He had been conductor of the Army No 2 Band based in Cork before he joined Radio Éireann in 1937. The first Army Bandmaster to be commissioned, he had written incidental music for a number of Abbey and Gate Theatre plays, and a select number of orchestral pieces. Duff was awarded a doctorate from Dublin University.

In 1943 Bowles had established Cór Radio Éireann, a small choral group of twenty-

8 June 1947
Capitol Theatre

Wagner: Overture, 'Die Meistersinger'
Brahms: Piano Concerto no 1
Larchet: Lament for Youth
Larchet: March, quasi scherzo
Mussorgsky/
Ravel: Pictures at an Exhibition

Julius Katchen, piano
Jean Martinon, conductor

22 June 1947
Capitol Theatre

Moeran: Rhapsody no 2
Haydn: Cello Concerto in D
Roussel: Festin de L'araignée
Beethoven: Symphony no 5

Paul Tortelier, cello
Jean Martinon, conductor

6 July 1947
Capitol Theatre

Mozart: Symphony no 40, K550
Mozart: Violin Concerto no 4, K218
Martinon: Concerto Giocoso
May: Scherzo
Ravel: La valse

Jean Fournier, violin
Jean Martinon, conductor

20 July 1947
Capitol Theatre

Harty: With the Wild Geese
Ravel: Piano Concerto
Roussel: Bacchus et Ariane
Brahms: Symphony no 4

Ginette Doyen, piano
Jean Martinon, conductor

7 December 1947
Capitol Theatre

Brahms: Tragic Overture
Brahms: Violin Concerto
D'Indy: Introduction to 'Fervaal'
Bartók: Concerto for Orchestra*
**First Irish performance*

André de Ribaupierre, violin
Edmond Appia, conductor

25 January 1948
Capitol Theatre

Pergolesi: Concertino no 2 for strings
Beethoven: Symphony no 7
Ina Boyle: Wild Geese
Lalo: Symphonie espagnole
Chabrier: Espana

Georges Tessier, violin
Edmond Appia, conductor

four voices. Again these were on a contract basis and Sir Hugh Roberton, conductor of the famous Glasgow Orpheus Choir, assisted in the auditions. The Cór included some illustrious personnel including Mary MacGoris, Leo Maguire, Sam Mooney and Tomás Roseingrave. Roberton conducted the Choir's first concert, attended by An Taoiseach, Éamon de Valera, on 25 June. As well as its separate studio broadcasts, the group joined the Orchestra for some of the smaller scale choral works, the Fauré *Requiem* and the 'Song of Destiny' by Brahms among them, and augmented other choirs in some of the larger oratorios.

The variety of the Orchestra's programmes is indicated by the programme for 29 October 1944 which consisted of Fleischmann's 'Four Masters' Overture, May's 'Spring Nocturne', Bowles's own 'Divertimento for strings', Moeran's Violin Concerto (with Nancie Lord) and Tchaikovsky's 'Pathétique' Symphony. This concert led to a letter to the *Evening Mail* on 4 November criticising its contemporary content:

> *A Chara - I would like to make a few comments on the present series of symphony concerts being given by the Radio Éireann Orchestra. In my opinion too much of the programmes is being given over to music by contemporary or modern composers. While being duly appreciative of the works of such men as Bax, Moeran, Ireland etc., I feel sure that the audiences at the concerts would prefer a little more of the great 18th and early 19th century masters. The next concert is indicative of what I mean. It consists of Beethoven's 'Pastoral' symphony and then works by Bax, Vaughan Williams, John Ireland and Walton. Surely this is not giving 'the ancients' a fair place in the programme. Moreover, if one of Michael Bowles's ideas is to popularise classical music, he should throw in some of the lighter stuff, e.g. Haydn, Rossini, Scarlatti, whose music, if not termed great, is at least very melodic at times. I hope when planning the next series of concerts 'the powers that be' will be a little more equable in choosing the works to be performed. M Ó Ceallaigh, 2 Plas Fingall, Sraid Pruise, Bla Cliath.*

The fiftieth public concert took place on 9 December 1945, with Charles Lynch playing Rachmaninov's Third Piano Concerto. Bowles conducted, offering Dvořák's Serenade for Strings to begin and Beethoven's 'Eroica' Symphony after the interval. The Radio Éireann Orchestra had also celebrated the centenary of Thomas Davis and the Young Ireland movement on 9 September 1945 when the main works were Fleischmann's 'Clare's Dragoons', with Michael O'Higgins and Joan Denise Moriarty (War-Pipes) and Harty's 'Irish Symphony.' Because of the fairly easy access of scores, Bowles introduced a number of works by Arnold Bax and Ralph Vaughan Williams to Irish audiences. Bax had lived in Dublin for almost two years from 1915 and returned as often as he could.

The end of the War brought a change in the musical life of Dublin. Continental European artists became available and Bowles was quick to bring to his concerts the French pianists Jeanne-Marie Darré, who played Beethoven's Fourth Concerto on 14 October 1945 and Monique Haas,

León Ó Broin

P J Little (Minister for Posts & Telegraphs)

who was heard in the Schumann Concerto on 13 October 1946. The soprano Oda Slobodskaya sang Isolde's 'Liebestod' on 27 October and Henry Holst returned to play the Sibelius Concerto in January 1947. Leon Goossens was heard in the Oboe Concerto of Richard Strauss in the same month.

Advent of Jean Martinon

Bowles also invited the very distinguished French conductor Charles Münch (who later took over the Boston Symphony Orchestra) to undertake a programme in March 1946. Münch was delighted but unfortunately illness forced him to cancel his planned appearance. He suggested his protegé, the young and highly talented violinist/conductor Jean Martinon, and this was accepted by Bowles and Radio Éireann.

Martinon had studied with Albert Roussel and Roger Désormière and was also a composer (his 'Stalag IX' was a musical impression of the prison camp in which he was held during the war. Martinon would introduce the work to Dublin on 18 September). He conducted in the Capitol on 31 March and his programme consisted of Mozart's 'Haffner' Symphony and Beethoven's Eighth, 'The Sorcerer's Apprentice' by Dukas and Debussy's 'La Mer'.

One of Martinon's June 1947 studio concerts was a memorial to Manuel de Falla who had died the previous November. The soloist in 'Nights in the Gardens of Spain' was Kitty O'Callaghan. Another June studio concert was devoted to French music, the main work being Roussel's Third Symphony, with Rhoda Coghill the soloist in the Franck Symphonic Variations. In October 1947 Martinon conducted the first performance of Aloys Fleischmann's song cycle 'The Fountain of Magic' with the soprano Violet Burne in a programme which also included Brahms's First Symphony.

Martinon made a considerable impression and in a way this had a major effect in general on matters musical in Radio Éireann and on Michael Bowles in particular.

Writing in the *RTÉ Guide* (12 March 1976) about Jean Martinon after his death on 1 March 1976 John O'Donovan commented:

> *Above all, he created the impression of a man who was the complete master of himself, whose head governed his heart, who shrank from sloppiness and who was too fastidious to play to the gallery. The women in the orchestra adored him and made no secret of it, but the rather shy smile, touched with sadness, inhibited the growth of jealousy in the men players. Besides, the men recognised his efficiency and knowledge of his craft. Thus he had the rare knack of being able, at one and the same time, to display his ability and to disarm the resentment that ability arouses at close quarters and he was second to none at fitting mailed fists with velvet gloves.*

The Minister for Posts and Telegraphs, under whose aegis Radio Éireann rested, was PJ Little. He was a cultured man with what might seem grandiose, but were in fact far-seeing, ideas. He had proposed an arts complex for Dublin, including a proper concert hall, devoted

Charles Lynch was one of the most popular and frequent soloists with the Orchestra

entirely to professional performances, for Dublin, plans and a model of which were actually prepared. The intended site was in the area of the Rotunda on Parnell Square. He had in mind instituting a Dublin orchestra, separate from Radio Éireann, which would enjoy a prestigious international reputation with a world-famous 'star' conductor in charge. He saw it rivalling those of London and Paris. That this proposal eventually came to nothing was neither the fault of Minister Little nor his supportive departmental Secretary, León Ó Broin.

One plan of Little's which did come to fruition was the setting up of a Summer School for young musicians. This enjoyed Department of Education and Radio Éireann approval and ran for a number of years from 1946. The School had its base in the Catering College in Cathal Brugha Street but the Phoenix Hall was used for the orchestral and conducting courses. The early visiting conductor-tutors were Jean Martinon, Louis Martin of Strasbourg Radio, Hans Schmidt-Isserstedt and Harry Mortimer (for wind bands). Students came from home and abroad and an early prestige attached itself to the venture. The first School, which attracted two hundred students to its various courses, was free, and travelling expenses were paid by the Department of Education, which granted £1,500 towards the costs.

However, while it was a hope that eventually a permanent conductor of a Radio Éireann Symphony Orchestra would be Irish, it would also seem that neither Michael Bowles nor JM Doyle was in the running. The issue was raised in 'An Irishman's Diary' in *The Irish Times* on 20 July 1949. The piece was critical of the fact that only two of the previous year's student conductors (one of whom was Brian Boydell who, as the writer pointed out, was already the conductor of the Dublin Orchestral Players) had actually been invited to conduct the Orchestra since then. It went on:

> *The Summer School of Music is now in its fourth year, and if so far it does not seem to have produced anyone likely to develop into a promising conductor, the explanation must be either the method of instruction is wrong or the wrong people are being chosen to take the course. There is a third possibility; that no latent conducting talent exists in Ireland.*

Fortunately in time this latter supposition would be proved inaccurate.

Creation of the Radio Éireann Symphony Orchestra

But Little and his departmental Secretary, León Ó Broin, also had an abiding interest in the Radio Éireann Orchestra. Coincidentally at this time (1946) Michael Bowles put forward the idea of enlarging it to sixty-five musicians (he had in mind an eventual figure of eighty) and establishing a Light Orchestra of some twenty-two players who would also augment the larger orchestra when the repertoire demanded. PJ Little fairly readily agreed to these proposals and to the idea of placing the orchestral musicians on a permanent footing (in line with another Bowles recommendation).

The upshot was that Government approval was given to increase the Orchestra to sixty-two, including a

Edmond Appia

pianist, and to establish a 'Light Orchestra' of twenty-two players. It was also considered essential to recruit from outside the country and to achieve this objective Michael Bowles was directed to travel throughout Europe and audition suitable candidates. Advertisements would also be placed in the national press and auditions held. The European auditions were arranged with the help and co-operation of the Department of External (Foreign) Affairs and local conservatoires and music academies.

Besides this, Bowles was also offered two years' paid leave of absence to advance his own conducting career. The idea was that a number of the European broadcasting stations would reciprocate by sending their conductors to direct the Dublin Orchestra. Part of this plan was indeed fulfilled, as Bowles himself had engaged the Swedish artist Sixten Eckerberg for Dublin and had appeared with Gothenburg's Radio Orchestra himself in December 1947. The same was true for both Rome and Brussels, and the Swiss musician Edmond Appia, who was Ernest Ansermet's assistant in the Geneva-based Suisse Romande Orchestra, also came to Dublin for a number of concerts during 1946-48.

Vincenzo Bellezza, who had conducted regularly in Rome, came in September 1947 for two concerts in the Theatre Royal with the soprano Gabriella Gatti as soloist. Respighi's 'Ancient Airs and Dances' (a work recently recorded for Naxos by the NSO) was on the first programme but as a harpsichord was unavailable in Dublin he insisted on tacks being inserted into the hammers on a piano instead. The resultant damage had severe consequences for the instrument. However in an interview with the *Sunday Independent* on 7 September 1947 Bellezza made the following point -

> *'In Italy today life is hard and money is scarce but musicians are well paid and good musicians are adequately paid. You (Irish) have great natural abilities; you should appreciate singers and musicians; but when you advertised recently for musicians you did not offer the salaries which would attract the best. Why?'*

Bowles's Resignation

What Bowles did not know, however, was that after his two years leave of absence he would return only as Director of Music without continuing as Conductor of the Orchestra. Innocently he went to Europe in the summer of 1947 visiting Paris, Lisbon, Rome, Berne and Brussels. He did sterling ground work and successfully completed part of his quest, namely, finding several highly suitable musicians for the enlarged Radio Éireann Orchestra. He returned to Dublin to see the new players settled in their unfamiliar environment and, as he thought, to conduct some concerts of the enlarged band before resuming his leave.

In his short absence, however, things had changed. Robert Brennan was Director of Broadcasting and Jean Martinon, who had no involvement with any radio orchestra in France, had been given a contract for a number of concerts in the spring of 1948. Indeed, at the end of Martinon's final 1947 concert on 31 October, which was in the Abbey Lecture Hall ('A Fugal Fantasy' by Leslie Seymour; Ravel's Left Hand Concerto,

with Claude Beche, and Messiaen's *L'Ascension*), Robert Brennan paid a public tribute to the conductor and spoke with the warmest appreciation of his magnificent work with the Radio Éireann Orchestra which he had brought to such a high standard in a few months. Robert Brennan said he understood arrangements were being made to invite Martinon to come back in February.

In replying, Martinon said it was difficult to work hard with an orchestra and remain friends with them. He hoped he had succeeded in doing both these things and he looked forward with pleasure to returning to Dublin.

Bowles was taken aback but his objections met with opposition and he was advised that if he did not comply with the terms of his 'leave of absence' he would be deemed to have relinquished his position. Michael Bowles, acting rather too hastily, offered his own resignation which was accepted.

The newspapers carried the story. *The Irish Times* of 15 January 1948 mentioned that 'Radio Éireann officials yesterday declined to give any information concerning the cause of his (Bowles) resignation'.

The Irish Times had this piece the next day:

> *The resignation of Captain M A Bowles from the post of Musical Director in Radio Éireann has been accepted. This information was given last night to an Irish Times reporter by Mr Robert Brennan, Director of Broadcasting.*
>
> *Asked about a successor being appointed to Captain Bowles Mr Brennan said "We have not got round to that yet". He explained that when Captain Bowles went abroad in June last the Radio Éireann authorities appointed Mr Fachtna Ó hAnnracháin in his place for a temporary period of two years. "This means" he said "that Mr Ó hAnnracháin has a year and a half to go".*
>
> *Captain Bowles yesterday said "I do not wish to discuss the reason for my resignation from Radio Éireann except to say that it is not of recent origin".*
>
> *Asked if he had any plans for the future he said "I have no immediate plans".*

The *Evening Herald* had another piece on 2 April:

> *Capt Michael Bowles, former musical director of Radio Éireann and conductor of the Radio Symphony Orchestra, left Shannon Airport today for Rome where he has been engaged to conduct a symphony concert for the Arts Society of the University of Rome. Capt Bowles, who will return to Dublin next week, denied rumours that he has plans to take up a musical appointment in Italy or Australia.*

A rehearsal in the Phoenix Hall

2

THE RTÉSO
1948-1973

Fachtna Ó hAnnracháin, then a young music teacher and choral conductor, had applied for the advertised position of Acting Music Director and joined Radio Éireann in June 1947. PJ Little was still Minister for Posts and Telegraphs with León Ó Broin the Department's Assistant Secretary. Both, as has been pointed out, had a keen interest in music, León being the father of Eimear Ó Broin who would, in time, become assistant conductor of the RÉSO. León Ó Broin, later Secretary of the Department, gave Fachtna Ó hAnnracháin every possible support in pursuing his duties.

Ó hAnnracháin recalls that being *'determined, in the interests of music, to implement the governmental authorization to have a symphony orchestra of sixty-two players and a light orchestra of twenty-two, but faced with the fact that Michael Bowles had not completed his quest for suitable orchestral players on the continent and the probability that some of those who had successfully auditioned for him might not accept an appointment in Radio Éireann, I had to satisfy myself that a sufficient number of musicians would be available to staff both orchestras.*

Fortunately I found that the existing pool of orchestral players in Radio Éireann, coupled with the continental musicians (from Belgium, Italy and Switzerland) who finally decided to accept positions in Dublin, and some free-lance Irish musicians who were available, would just about provide enough orchestral players to enable both orchestras to be established, and I obtained the approval of the authorities in Radio Éireann and the Department of Posts and Telegraphs to proceed accordingly'.

Phoenix Hall

When postal censorship came to an end after the War, the building in which this activity (along with mail sorting) was carried out - the Phoenix Hall in Dame Court, between Dame Street and Exchequer Street - became free. The hall acquired its name from its hurried construction to enable the Irish Hospitals Sweepstakes to accommodate its staff and continue trading when its original premises at the old Plaza Cinema were destroyed by fire. As it happened, the Department of Posts and Telegraphs was erecting new premises on an adjacent site in Exchequer Street which it had purchased before the war and which would be used mainly as the Telephone Exchange. Quite soon the nearby hall would have an important role in Dublin's musical life.

When the Sweepstakes moved to its new premises in Ballsbridge the Department, took over the Phoenix Hall next-door for use by the Radio Éireann Orchestra. Fitted out in time as a studio to hold a full

Renzo Marchionni

During his time in Dublin Renzo Marchionni gave a number of memorable concerto performances with the Orchestra. The first of these was the Bach Double with Zola Cirulli on 21 January 1949 under Sixten Eckerberg. He played the Brahms in Dublin, Cork, Limerick and Waterford in the week commencing 14 February 1954. These were followed by the Brahms Double with Maurice Meulien, then the RÉSO's principal cellist, on June 18 1954 under Milan Horvat in the Phoenix Hall. This was repeated in the Gaiety on 20 January 1957 but in between Beethoven's Triple Concerto with Meulien and Anthony Hughes came to the Metropolitan Hall with Horvat conducting on 8 July 1955. Marchionni played Paganini's First Concerto in the Olympia Theatre at a 'Prom' on 16 October 1955.

symphony orchestra, it would also seat an audience of 300-400. Before, and for a while after, the musicians occupied it, the Phoenix Hall also acted as a kind of quartermaster's store and held thousands of army blankets and mattresses. These were piled high and one of the musicians' first tasks was to cope with a plague of fleas which had found comfortable accommodation in the bedding.

The Hall was officially opened by Minister Little on 30 January 1948 (although it had been used for many studio broadcasts by the Orchestra since 1946). This was in fact the last concert by the old Radio Éireann Orchestra and was conducted by Edmond Appia. The soloist in Grieg's Piano Concerto was Patricia Herbert and the main work was Schumann's First Symphony. The musicians wore evening dress.

One press report mentioned the décor as 'tastefully coloured in biscuit and a fascinating light blue-green' which the writer found 'hard to define'. Another wrote

> *'The new hall, which has been specially planned for broadcast concerts, is designed to give that resonant and live quality of sound that is essential to any concert, whether broadcast or not. The effect of the orchestra, both over the air and in the hall itself, is excellent'.*

The new orchestra was established from February 1948 and among the continental players recruited by Michael Bowles, and who had been gathering in Dublin from late 1947, was the Florentine violinist Renzo Marchionni. The leader of the Radio Éireann Orchestra, until her resignation at the end of 1945, had been Waterford-born Terry O'Connor. In the intervening period up to 1948 the position was held by Nancie Lord, who co-operated fully with Marchionni's appointment. He was chosen as leader, his qualities being recognised by Bowles as soon as he came into his audition in Rome. Marchionni's appointment - he was the first man to lead the Orchestra - was fortuitous as he proved to be a highly accomplished musician, as well as a very agreeable and affable person who endeared himself to musicians and audiences alike. His initial salary was £11 per week with a £3 disturbance allowance. He held his position until 1959 when family reasons forced his return to Florence.

A number of other Italian string players joined the new orchestra, among them Zola Cirulli, who later established the Cirulli Ensemble, Lamberto ("Luigi") Corbara and Alfonso Evangelisti in the violins, with viola players Wilson Formica and Mario Gavagnin. Cellist Lucien de Groot was Belgian, as were principal horn Leopold Laurent, and principal oboe Léon Thonon. The principal trombone, Novemo Salvadori, hailed from Italy, while Gernot Essig, another member of the horn section, was Swiss, as was Suzi Luthi in the first violins.

Among the Irish members in the RÉSO in 1948 were Alice Brough, Rosalind Dowse, Marie Lillis Condron, Nancie Lord, Joan McElroy, Peggy Kelaghan (wife of Kevin Roche), Carmel Lang, Madeleine Mooney, James Chapman, Chris Kiernan and William Shanahan in the violins. The violas included Máire Larchet, Tom Collins and Ferruccio Grossi, a long-established Irish resident; the cellos had Nancy Doyle, Christine Fagan, Kathleen

Arthur Nachstern

Arthur Nachstern was born in Odessa of Polish parentage, and studied at the Conservatoire there under Peter Stolarski, the teacher of Milstein and Heifetz. Having returned to Poland, he studied at the Warsaw Conservatoire where he, Witold Lutoslawski, Andrzej Panufnik and Witold Malcuzynski were known as the Four Musketeers. He was professor at the Music Academy of Karlowicza in Warsaw and a member of the Warsaw Philharmonic, later joining the Santa Cecilia Orchestra in Rome. After coming to the RÉSO in 1947, he played Paganini's concerto no 1 under Appia, and in June 1951 the Glazunov Concerto, which he had performed in Odessa with the composer conducting. He recalls: 'the achievements of the early years of the RÉSO laid a firm foundation for what we know today as the National Symphony Orchestra. Looking back, we were very fortunate: as a country we were small, musically we were not known internationally, yet such a wealth of brilliant conductors and musicians – some of them world-famous – were coming to Ireland and giving us the benefit of their experience.'

Pollaky and Clyde Twelvetrees. Robert Bushnell and Zack Lee were in the double-bass line up, with Kevin Roche joining some months later.

There were flautists Tom Browne and Herbert Leeming, with clarinettists Freddy Ashton and Adolf Gebler, an Austrian musician who had come to Dublin in the 1930s as part of a visiting ensemble and remained. Other wind players were Joe Murphy, oboe/cor anglais and Richard Persse with PJ Donnelly, bassoons.

The brass included horns Harry Woods and Nick Gibbons; Herbert Treacy, Joseph Cassells and Charles Parkes (who had previously played in the Theatre Royal,) trumpets; Harry Thwaites and Paddy Feeney, trombones and Tommy Dunne, tuba; Stanislaus (Ossie) Stack, timpani, and Pat O'Regan, percussion. Husband and wife duo Dora and Walter Hall sat in the violin and viola desks.

Another artist who had come to Dublin separately after the war was the Odessa-born Polish violinist, Arthur Nachstern. He had been accepted into the Radio Éireann Orchestra as soon as he presented himself for audition in 1947. He was to remain until his retirement on reaching the age limit in 1976 and continued in a deputy capacity until 1992. He was deputy leader for a lengthy period and took over the leader's chair many times.

There were also a number of 'extras' who were not yet on the permanent roll-call. In time this would lead to a 'union issue' and Dáil questions. Salaries had increased to £8 per week for men and £7.10s for women. The 'extras' received £7 and £6.10s respectively.
But the matter of continental musicians had not gone without derogatory comment from the Irish Federation of Musicians. It ran a national newspaper advertisement between 30 January and 2 February 1948: -

RADIO "ÉIREANN" ORCHESTRA

* *The Minister of Industry and Commerce says, "Full employment is our goal"*
* *The Minister for Posts and Telegraphs, Mr PJ Little gives preference to foreigners*
* *He is concerned for our cultural standards, but ignores the standard of living.*
* *He displaces Irish Musicians and replaces them with displaced foreigners.*

Why are foreigners being imported to make an "Irish" Orchestra ? Why ?

Replying to this criticism while on a visit to Waterford, Minister PJ Little was reported in the *Irish Independent* on 2 February and the *Waterford Standard* on 7 February as saying:

'The introduction of foreign musicians had been an absolute necessity only resorted to after all their own musicians had been sought. The broadcasting authorities had sought to employ every Irish musician competent to pass the examinations set by experts and there was a considerable number of vacancies for those willing to submit to examination and who were able to pass the test.

In 1939 the orchestra consisted of 28 players and the (annual) cost was £7,500. In 1943 the number was increased to 40. The new Symphony

André Prieur

Gilbert Berg

Albert Solivérès

Maurice Meulien

Orchestra now had 62 players and the Light Orchestra 22 players. The cost for 1947/48 was estimated to be £33,000; salaries had increased by 50 per cent, holidays with pay had been increased, payment during sick leave had been added and gratuities on retirement would be given.

The Federation was not entirely satisfied with this ministerial response.

The disturbance allowance, £3 per week in the case of married men and £2 for single people, caused some contention the following year. The *Irish Times* Dáil Report of 16 June 1949 had the following from Deputy M Fitzpatrick:

Irish instrumentalists should be paid the same rate as foreign ones - otherwise they will continue to be bitterly resentful. Temporary appointments should be made permanent and young people encouraged to regard music as a secure and honourable profession. Public concerts should be restarted, not only in Dublin but in the provinces where there is a terrible dearth of music. There seems no reason why the symphony and the light orchestras should not spend even a few weeks of the year on tour.

After the initial influx of continental musicians a number of others came to Dublin, among them the French flautist Christian Lardé in 1949 and Roland Dufrane who replaced Léon Thonon. Lardé later joined the Paris Conservatoire Orchestra and was followed in 1950 by another very fine French artist, André Prieur, who remained as principal flautist for many years. Prieur was one of the founders and conductor of the original Irish Chamber Orchestra and the leader of the highly accomplished Prieur Instrumental Ensemble - one of the several chamber music groups formed by members of the RÉSO with Radio Éireann's blessing.

The year 1949 also brought Wolfram Henschel from Germany as principal cellist and Raymond Malfait to be principal clarinet. Another remarkable Frenchman, Gilbert Berg, became principal bassoon. His *Les Amis de la Musique* was another of those celebrated chamber music groups which emerged from RÉSO ranks. Indeed an official Radio Éireann Wind Quintet was instituted in September 1949 consisting of Christian Lardé, Roland Dufrane, Raymond Malfait, Gilbert Berg and Leopold Laurent.

French cellist Maurice Meulien arrived in Dublin the following year to lead the section. This he did with refined sensitivity until moving to the London Symphony Orchestra in 1966. The Algerian-born Albert Solivérès entered the orchestra as its exceptionally fine principal oboe in 1952. Now retired, he continues to reside in Dublin.

The double-bass line was enhanced by Rudolf Frei and later by Willy Clasen, Heinz Jablonski and Edmund Nowak, who was later joined by his brother Herbert. In time, Clasen went to the Zagreb Philharmonic and the Yugoslav, Jablonski, who married the violinist Monica Maguire, joined the Deutsche Oper in Berlin.

One of the beneficial side-effects of employing the continental musicians was

Jean Meylan

Jean Martinon

their availability to teach privately and in Dublin's two major music schools - the Royal Irish Academy of Music and the Municipal School of Music. León Ó Broin, who hoped for the eventual establishment of a conservatoire in Dublin, in fact negotiated the employment of the émigré musicians with the RIAM, as a way of supplementing their Radio Éireann salaries.

But to return to 1948, through Fachtna Ó hAnnracháin's initiative and persuasiveness it was agreed that the RÉSO would give two weekly live broadcasts on fixed days - rather than on varying days - from the Phoenix Hall with an invited audience in attendance. Tuesday and Friday were the days chosen, with Tuesday's one-hour programme and the first half of Friday's, also an hour, transmitted directly. The second part of the Friday concert was recorded for later broadcasting. This 'set days' decision became effective from May 1948.

Concert programmes could be fairly adventurous and, as they were not restricted by box-office demands, the repertoire was wide-ranging, with a considerable input of contemporary music on offer. The new Orchestra's second concert on 20 February, for instance, included the first Dublin performance of Walton's Viola Concerto with Frederick Riddle.

But the early months of 1948 also brought changes to Dáil Éireann. Fianna Fáil had been defeated in a general election and an inter-party government had James Everett as Minister for Posts and Telegraphs. Following severe financial constraints in a number of areas, the idea of 'public' concerts by the Radio Éireann Orchestras could not be countenanced. Moreover, Everett announced that as a matter of policy he would not employ 'foreigners or non-nationals' in Radio Éireann.

The concerts were now considered to be a financial liability and of course needed the approval of both the Departments of Posts and Telegraphs and Finance for them to continue. The idea of dropping them aroused a good deal of criticism then and later, with devotees of Michael Bowles believing that the Phoenix Hall concerts could not be a proper substitute for the old concerts in either the Mansion House or Capitol. Bowles indeed issued a statement on the matter as well as a short letter to the *Irish Independent* of 8 June 1948 as follows:

> *Sir - I have been reliably informed that owing to the economy campaign, the Radio Éireann Public Symphony Concerts are being abandoned - certainly for the 1948/49 season, and possibly for some years to come. I think this would be a pity. From my six years experience of Dublin audiences I would venture to suggest that such concerts would not be an intolerable drain on the exchequer, if, indeed, they would cost anything at all.*
>
> *Besides it may reasonably be considered a waste of a large and expensive orchestra to confine it to studio performances before an invited audience of 300 or so.*

From Radio Éireann's point of view the Phoenix Hall was an ideal solution to an old problem. A radio orchestra's first duty was to its radio listeners, but on the other hand it could not be expected to play

15 October 1948
Abbey Lecture Hall

Haydn:	Symphony no 92 ('Oxford')
Vaughan Williams:	Oboe Concerto
Franck:	Symphony in D minor

Léon Thonon, oboe
Hans Schmidt-Isserstedt, conductor

29 October 1948
Phoenix Hall

Duff:	Irish Suite for strings
Rawsthorne:	Piano Concerto no 1
Mozart:	Symphony no 40, K550

James Gibb, piano
Hans Schmidt-Isserstedt, conductor

18 September 1949
City Hall, Cork

Beethoven:	Symphony no 3 ('Eroica')
Schubert:	Entr'actes from 'Rosamunde'
Rachmaninov:	Rhapsody on a theme of Paganini
Wagner:	Overture, 'Die Meistersinger'

Charles Lynch, piano
Hans Schmidt-Isserstedt, conductor

Hans Schmidt-Isserstedt

permanently to a studio's blank walls and microphones. Concerts to a paying public could cause a good deal of dislocation and deflect the choice of programmes in the direction of the box-office. They could also provide less than satisfactory broadcasting, technically and programmatically, for listeners at home.

The Music Association of Ireland, founded in 1948 by a number of luminaries - Olive Smith, Brian Boydell, Edgar Deale and Michael McMullin among them - raised the issue of public concerts with Radio Éireann towards the end of that year and again in both 1949 and 1950. The MAI had itself attempted to arrange a number of concerts with the Orchestra, and at one stage the Department offered to allow the Association take over the running of the public concerts.

The Department argued that a loss of over £100 [£1500 today] had been incurred on each concert in 1947, exclusive of the cost of salaries. This loss was outside the ordinary expenditure on broadcasting and could not be justifiably met from broadcasting funds. The MAI could not however condone losing this kind of money out of its limited resources either, and efforts to enlist the help of the management of the Capitol also failed. Negotiations with Dublin Corporation for the Round Room in the Mansion House also came to nothing and in the long run public symphony concerts in Dublin were put on the back burner for the time being.

The initial 'invitation' concert of the new RÉSO took place on 14 February 1948 in the Phoenix Hall under the baton of Jean Martinon. The programme included Brahms's Academic Festival Overture, Fauré's *'Masques et Bergamasques'* and the symphonic suite *Mathis der Maler* by Paul Hindemith. Martinon remained as guest conductor for three months, giving a Debussy programme on 25 March commemorating the thirtieth anniversary of the composer's death.

Martinon was followed by the English musician Mosco Carner. Some of his programmes were highly adventurous and included Mahler's *Kindertotenlieder* with baritone Robert Irwin, and Dallapiccola's 'Piccolo' Concerto with the Hungarian pianist Ilona Kabos. Carner also gave a number of radio talks and it was he who had introduced Shostakovich's First Symphony to Irish audiences in a studio concert on 14 March 1947.

Martinon returned to premiere his Third (Irish) Symphony on 9 July 1948 and that month saw concerts by Swedish conductor Sixten Eckerberg, a man well versed in the problems of live music broadcasts, who introduced a number of Scandinavian works to Irish audiences.

The autumn of 1948 saw the arrival in Dublin for a number of concerts of Hans Schmidt-Isserstedt. Hamburg-based, he was another veteran of live music broadcasting, having conducted the North West German Radio Orchestra since its post-war inauguration.

Edmond Appia, who had conducted a number of concerts with the old RÉO soon after the war, came to the Phoenix Hall in November 1948 and the Italian conductor Francesco Mander, then based in Rome, made his Irish début with Dvořák's New World' Symphony in

18 February 1949
Phoenix Hall

Khachaturian: Piano Concerto
Roussel: Symphony no 3
Dukas: The Sorcerer's Apprentice

Charles Lynch, piano
Jean Fournet, conductor

1 July 1949
Phoenix Hall

Beethoven: Overture, Leonora no 3
Brahms: Symphony no 1

Carlo Zecchi, conductor

5 July 1949
Phoenix Hall

Tchaikovsky: Serenade
Tchaikovsky: Fantasy-overture, Romeo and Juliet

Carlo Zecchi, conductor

8 July 1949
Phoenix Hall

Schubert: Overture 'Rosamunde'
Schubert: Symphony no 9

Carlo Zecchi, conductor

December 1948. In one of his few appearances on the RÉSO rostrum Fachtna Ó hAnnracháin conducted the suitably seasonal Bach *Christmas Oratorio* in Christmas week that year.

Writing in the *Radio Éireann Year Book* for 1948 Ó hAnnracháin commented:

> *'Undoubtedly the most significant development for Radio Éireann during 1948, as far as music is concerned, was the formation of the Symphony and Light Orchestras in place of one orchestra which had existed up to then. Although it has not been found possible yet to bring both orchestras up to the full strength envisaged, nevertheless, the availability of two orchestras in place of one opened up great possibilities in the orchestral field. It was now possible for the larger orchestra to devote its whole time to symphonic music, and anyone who listened to the many concerts broadcast by this body of musicians during 1948, under the various guest conductors, will readily admit the great improvement in standards that took place both in the programmes and in the general standard of performance.*
>
> *Since the inauguration of these bi-weekly concerts many thousands have availed themselves of the opportunity of seeing and hearing the first permanent Irish Symphony Orchestra; and we have no doubt that these studio concerts will increase greatly the number of lovers of the world's great music.*
>
> *Both the Radio Éireann Symphony Orchestra and the Radio Éireann Light Orchestra are yet in their infancy, and a long road lies ahead. In all modesty, however, it may be said that the formative stage has been completed with success'.*

Tickets for the Phoenix Hall concerts were obtained through written application but this did not deter an ever-interested band of music lovers.

Sixten Eckerberg returned to conduct the RÉSO in January 1949 and on the recommendation of Jean Martinon another excellent French artist, the elegant Jean Fournet, took the Phoenix Hall rostrum in February.

The matter of visiting conductors was raised in Dáil Éireann in July 1949 and in a reply Minister Everett said that between 1 January 1948 and 30 June 1949 twelve foreign conductors had been engaged for the Radio Éireann Symphony Orchestra. Fees paid to them were £2,715.11s. In addition travel expenses totalling £288.10s.4d were paid to six conductors.

Appearance of Milan Horvat

A return visit of the Swiss conductor Rudolf F Denzler of Zurich Opera, who had conducted the RÉO in April 1947, occupied the RÉSO's programmes in June 1949. The renowned Hungarian pianist, Geza Anda, played the Liszt First and Beethoven 'Emperor' Concertos with him on 7 and 10 June. In November that year, again through the good offices of Jean Martinon, a young Yugoslav musician, Milan Horvat of Zagreb Radio, made his Irish début. His first programme on 2 November included Glinka's *Ruslan and Ludmilla* Overture, Tchaikovsky's 'Romeo and Juliet' and Dvořák's 'New World' Symphony.

In his other programmes Horvat's soloists were the emerging Irish virtuoso Anthony

2 February 1951
Phoenix Hall

Mozart: Symphony no 40, K550
Beethoven: Symphony no 3 ('Eroica')

Albert van Raalte, conductor

9 March 1951
Phoenix Hall

Schumann: Cello Concerto
Brahms: Symphony no 1

Paul Tortelier, cello
Albert van Raalte, conductor

24 March 1951
St Patrick's College, Maynooth

Rossini: Overture, 'The Thieving Magpie'
Mendelssohn: Violin Concerto
Beethoven: Symphony no 6 ('Pastoral')

François d'Albert, violin
Albert van Raalte, conductor

Hughes (Mozart's D minor Piano Concerto), Francois d'Albert (Beethoven's Violin Concerto) and Antonio Janigro (Haydn's C major Cello Concerto). He was himself the piano soloist in Bach's Fifth Brandenburg Concerto with Renzo Marchionni and Christian Lardé on 25 November. (A Dolmetsch harpsichord was purchased in 1951 and inaugurated by John Beckett in Handel's Concerto Grosso No 12 on 4 January 1952. Thurston Dart gave the first recital on it three days later). Horvat introduced a number of pieces to Ireland for the first time, with Stjepan Sulek's Second Symphony being the main work in his last concert on 2 December 1949. Although he did not return to Ireland again for about a year, Horvat would later be an important figure in Irish musical life.

Visiting conductors, German Otto Matzerath, Swiss Jean Meylan with Martinon, Fournet and Horvat among them, continued to keep the RÉSO musicians actively employed during 1950. A new Steinway piano was inaugurated by the American pianist Vera Francesci and Martinon with McDowell's D minor Piano Concerto on 14 April.

Otto Matzerath, who came from Karlsruhe, went with the RÉSO to Galway for a concert in aid of the Irish Red Cross on 4 September 1950 before an audience of over a thousand. He conducted a special concert on 10 September in the Capitol, the first time the theatre had been used as a concert venue since 1948, for delegates to the Inter-Parliamentary Union meeting in Dublin, and on 29 September Matzerath directed Bach's B minor Mass with the Culwick Choral Society and Cór Radio Éireann in the Metropolitan Hall. This performance, then unique in Dublin, commemorated the bicentenary of the composer's death and the concert was promoted in association with the MAI. The soloists were Margaret Field Hyde, Anne Wood, Ronald Bristol and Owen Brannigan.

The Dutch conductor, Albert van Raalte, gave a number of programmes with the Orchestra in the spring of 1951.

Martinon had already taken the Orchestra to Maynooth (8 April 1950 - Haydn's 'Clock' Symphony and Harty's 'With the Wild Geese' in the main) and Edmond Appia had previously directed the Orchestra in Holy Cross College, Clonliffe, in music by de Lalande and at Loreto College on Dublin's St Stephen's Green on 23 December 1949 in a seasonal programme that included a Pergolesi Mass. Concerts by the RÉSO in Dublin's Universities would come some time later. The Aula Maxima of UCD on St Stephen's Green was tried by Carlo Zecchi in November 1950 but during rehearsals it was decided the acoustics were unsuitable and the actual concert took place in the Phoenix Hall.

While not yet employed in giving public concerts of its own, the RÉSO had, almost since its inception, been engaged by outside bodies. Since its foundation in 1941, the Dublin Grand Opera Society had used the old RÉO for its Spring and Winter Seasons at the Gaiety Theatre, although initially this was on a free-lance basis with the blessing of Radio Éireann. Difficulties arose in 1944 and led to considerable controversy, and RÉ

Milan Horvat

Later Milan Horvat worked regularly with Austrian Radio and the Zagreb Philharmonic and, more recently still, conducted the music for the highly successful film, *Shine,* based on the life of the Australian pianist David Helfgott.

3 October 1948
Capitol Theatre
Verdi: Requiem

Lidia Cremona, soprano
Gilda Alfano, contralto
Manfredi Ponz de Léon, tenor
Alfredo Colella, bass

Our Lady's Choral Society
Jean Martinon, conductor

the Verdi Requiem was repeated on 21 April 1950 at the Phoenix Hall with

Veronica Dunne, soprano
Patricia Lawlor, contralto
Joseph McNally, tenor
Michael O'Higgins, bass

musicians did not have Radio Éireann's blessing to play for the opera company again until March 1946.

Things changed somewhat with the establishment of the RÉSO. Two categories of operation were put in place, (a) in co-operation with Radio Éireann where the musicians were paid by RÉ, and (b) where the musicians played on a free-lance basis. Radio Éireann had the option, however, to record both categories for later transmission.

This policy ran for a number of seasons until on one occasion the musicians refused to play for one of the category (b) operas and it seemed likely that the performance would be cancelled. Only the combined skill of the Gaiety's impresario Louis Elliman, Fachtna Ó hAnnracháin and Lt Col. Bill O'Kelly of the DGOS saved the day from disaster and from then on it was decided the free-lance position would end and Radio Éireann would assume responsibility for the Orchestra's entire operatic involvement. One of the first RÉSO/DGOS operas was Debussy's *Pelléas et Mélisande* in an Opéra-Comique Paris production conducted by Roger Désormière in the Spring of 1948. With Irene Joachim, Marguerite Myrtal, Henri Etcheverry and Jacques Jansen in the cast, it is still remembered with awe and affection by many who saw it.

For its Spring Seasons of 1950 and 1951 the DGOS had the good fortune of bringing productions from the Hamburg State Opera to the Gaiety, in which the RÉSO were involved. Arthur Grüber conducted *Don Giovanni* and *Cosí fan tutte* on the first visit and *The Barber of Seville* and *The Abduction from the Seraglio* in 1951. Grüber conducted a number of concerts with the Orchestra as well.

Opera would play an important part in the Orchestra's working life for the next forty years. It would give invaluable support to the DGOS performances in Dublin (Christmas and Easter) and Cork until 1991,when a change in artistic policy would reallocate the operatic role to the RTÉ Concert Orchestra. And, as we shall see, the Symphony Orchestra became - and remains - the backbone of the Wexford Opera Festival; in fact, at the height of its involvement with the three opera seasons in Dublin, Cork and Wexford, almost a third of its annual schedule would be dedicated to opera.

Besides the DGOS the RÉSO was also engaged by such bodies as Our Lady's Choral Society - a choir formed in 1945 and which inadvertently contributed to the demise of the well established Dublin Oratorio Society - for its annual Christmas *Messiah* performances and other choral ventures during the year. Indeed on 30 March 1947 Jean Martinon had conducted the choir and RÉO in a rare performance of César Franck's *The Beatitudes* in the Capitol.

Fachtna Ó hAnnracháin as Director of Music

It was the policy of Fachtna Ó hAnnracháin, who had become Director of Music in December 1949, to support Irish soloists as much as possible. Primary among these was pianist Charles Lynch who made regular appearances with the orchestra in a very varied repertoire from the classical, romantic and

THE IRISH TIMES and RTÉ

Music in the Classroom

contemporary fields. The pianists' roster also included Rhoda Coghill, who followed Kitty O'Callaghan as Radio Éireann's official accompanist, Patricia Herbert, who married Eimear Ó Broin, Anthony Hughes, Florence Ryan and Gerard Shanahan.

The violin soloists included Mary Gallagher, Margaret Hayes, Geraldine O'Grady, John Ronayne and Jaroslav Vaneček. This Czech-born artist had come to Ireland to give a recital with his wife at the Royal Dublin Society and asked to remain in the country. His first post was at the Royal Irish Academy of Music but he then moved to Dublin's Municipal School of Music where he was violin professor for many years. (Vaneček constantly showed a fatherly concern for his pupils' welfare and if several of his pupils became distinguished members of the orchestra - among them Mary Gallagher, Margaret Hayes, Timothy Kirwan, Clodagh McSwiney and of course the incredible Audrey Park - this was only after he was fully satisfied that the right time had arrived for them to embark on a professional career.) Irish singers included Veronica Dunne, Maura O'Connor, Austin Gaffney and Michael O'Higgins, while leaders of the various orchestral departments would often appear under the soloist's spotlight.

Children's concerts introduced

Although schools broadcasts had been a feature of the music schedules for several years, the year 1951 also saw the first Children's Concerts when Hubert Clifford conducted and introduced two programmes at the Phoenix Hall on 3 April. The following year brought the formation of Ceol-chumann na nÓg, the Children's Concerts Association. This came through the efforts of the Department of Education and Sir Robert and Lady Dorothy Mayer. Sir Robert had started a children's concerts programme in London and Lady Mayer had an Irish background. Indeed she later agreed to contribute £150 per annum towards the expense of an organiser and James Blanc was appointed to this post in 1952.

The Cumann's first official concerts were held in the Phoenix Hall on the morning of 5 February 1952. Girls attended at 10am, boys at 11am with Hubert Clifford, who had been closely involved with the Mayers' work in England, conducting in the presence of Lady Mayer. The Minister for Education attended the concert on 1 April 1952 when Arthur Duff conducted and the Department's Music Inspector, Peadar Ó Cillín, introduced the programme.

The concerts were later extended to the Orchestra's touring venues, with the children's programmes usually taking place on the morning following the public event. Some Ceol-chumann na nÓg concerts also took place at the Capitol in Dublin where at one of them Prokofiev's 'Peter and the Wolf' was narrated in Irish by Siobhán McKenna. By the end of November 1952 some seven thousand children had attended these concerts, and many more from 1968 experienced the Schools Recitals Scheme administered by the MAI which was made possible by the orchestral players' presence at regional venues. The Schools' Concerts continue as of the Orchestra's educational policy, supported today by *The Irish Times*. Together with *Music in the Classroom* and the RTÉ Concert Orchestra's *Music*

Hans Waldemar Rosen, founder of the RTÉ Singers, RTÉ's chamber choir which succeeded Cór Radio Éireann

The RTÉ Singers, pictured in 1965: from left **Mabel McGrath, Gerald Duffy, Mary Sheridan, Patricia Hanley, Daniel Murray, Minnie Clancy, Angela Carroll, Dr H W Rosen, Bene McAteer, Patrick Ring, Peter McBrien.**

for Fun concerts, they have introduced hundreds of thousands of young people (and their parents) to a taste of classical music and a chance to pursue further courses of musical appreciation.

Choral music

1952 also saw the inauguration of the amateur Radio Éireann Choral Society and its first rehearsal took place on 18 February that year. Its director was the Leipzig-born musician Hans Waldemar Rosen whose influence on Radio Éireann's phenomenal vocal music output would last many years. The choir's first performance with the RÉSO, conducted by Dr Rosen, was in Schumann's *Paradise and the Péri* on 24 April 1952. The soloists were Clothilde Johnston and Dermot Troy.

Its repertoire remained for the most part eclectic (Handel's *L'Allegro, Il penseroso ed Il moderato* for the bicentenary of the composer's death, Stravinsky's Symphony of Psalms under the composer's direction, the premiere of Brian Boydell's *'Mors et Vita'*, Gerard Victory's 'The Rivers of Heaven', Liszt's 'Faust' Symphony, Hindemith's 'When Lilacs last in the Door-yard bloom'd' and Anthony Milner's 'The Fire and the Water' are just a minute example) in order to avoid clashes with the other Dublin-based choral societies which might be relying on box office appeal for their performances. The RÉ (later RTÉ) Choral Society continued until 1984 when it was disbanded. Reconstituted as the RTÉ Philharmonic Choir under the direction of Colin Mawby in 1985, it continues to play a vital role in the musical life of RTÉ.

A smaller choral body, the Radio Éireann Singers, also with Hans Waldemar Rosen as its Conductor, came into being in 1953. It and the larger Choral Society supplanted Cór Radio Éireann. Initially its members were on a five year contract but this was later extended to an indefinite period. The group's repertoire was extraordinarily extensive as Hans Waldemar Rosen, and after him Proinnsías Ó Duinn, Eric Sweeney and Colin Mawby, had unusually wide horizons in their choice of music. The Singers, who gave innumerable first performances of both native and foreign composers, had very many engagements with the Orchestra until their eventual disbanding in 1984. The library of the Singers, which is today at the disposal of the National Chamber Choir, is a huge and invaluable resource of Irish and international music, containing much work commissioned from Irish composers and arrangers such as Redmond Friel and Eamonn Ó Gallchobhair.

Another development was the formation of a training orchestra in 1953. The purpose here was to prepare young Irish musicians for an ultimate position in the RÉSO. The group met in the Radio Éireann studios in Portobello (which was also the home of the Light Orchestra) once a week under the direction of Eimear Ó Broin and Jaroslav Vaneček. Despite the relatively short life of this group (1953-57), it may have sown the seeds for the eventual emergence of the Irish Youth Orchestra.

The 1950s were a period too when the supporters of Dublin's Adelaide Hospital organised a series of celebrity concerts and recitals at the Theatre Royal in Hawkins Street - like the Capitol, long

20 February 1953
Phoenix Hall

Mendelssohn:	Overture, 'A Midsummer Night's Dream'
Mahler:	Symphony no 4*

Celestine Kelly, soprano
Winfried Zillig, conductor
First performance in Ireland

22 March 1953
Gaiety Theatre

Tchaikovsky programme

Fantasy-overture, Romeo and Juliet
Piano Concerto no 1
Symphony no 6 ('Pathétique')

France Ellegaard, piano
Winfried Zillig, conductor

27 March 1953
Phoenix Hall

Berg:	Three excerpts from 'Wozzeck'
Schoenberg:	Chamber Symphony no 1
Zillig:	'The Nearness of the Beloved'

Ilse Zeyen, soprano
Winfried Zillig, conductor

24 July 1953
Phoenix Hall

Mozart:	Les petits riens K.anh 19
Mozart:	Piano Concerto no 21 in C, K467
Stenhammer:	Interlude - Mellanspiel ur Kantaten 'Sangen' op44
Sibelius:	Symphony no 7

Ginette Doyen, piano
Sixten Eckerberg, conductor

11 September 1953
Phoenix Hall

Gluck:	Ballet suite, 'Orfeo ed Euridice'
Tchaikovsky:	Piano Concerto no 1
Brahms:	Symphony no 4

Shulamith Shafir, piano
Milan Horvat, piano

since demolished. Among the earliest of these involving the RÉSO were concerts with the Australian pianist Eileen Joyce, who played the Grieg and Schumann Concertos with Milan Horvat conducting on 27 January 1951, and the Polish pianist Witold Malcuzinski in Liszt's Second Concerto on 14 July 1951 under the baton of Jean Meylan.

Miss Joyce was a very popular soloist who liked to change her frocks to suit her music but Mr Horvat felt a programme with two concertos rather reduced the importance of the orchestra and made it known he was not over pleased with the idea. The violin virtuoso Joseph Szigeti also took part in one of these 'Adelaide' concerts in 1 March 1952 under Otto Matzerath. The programme was mainly the Beethoven Concerto and Schumann's Fourth Symphony and the attendance included the President of Ireland and Mrs Seán T O'Kelly. Louis Kentner played the 'Emperor' and Liszt E flat Concertos on 28 February 1953 under Winfried Zillig while Benno Moisewitsch was heard in Beethoven's Third Piano Concerto under Horvat on 27 February 1954. Illness prevented his performance of Rachmaninov's Paganini Rhapsody as well.

Reinstatement of public concerts - Gaiety Theatre

Radio Éireann now felt it was time to approach the Department of Posts and Telegraphs on the matter of public concerts in Dublin. The response was not immediate but in due course the 1948 decision was reversed and Fachtna Ó hAnnracháin set about organising a series of Sunday concerts in Dublin's Gaiety Theatre for early January 1953. The choice of day was determined by the theatre management but was not altogether favourable to the musicians. They had become accustomed to having their week-ends free and being now obliged to rehearse on Saturdays and perform on Sundays was not entirely to their liking. However, agreement was reached and, with the French conductor Pierre Michel le Conte on the rostrum, the first of these somewhat fancifully named 'Prom' concerts took place on 11 January 1953. The soloist in Rachmaninov's Second Concerto was Charles Lynch and later soloists included soprano Gwen Catley, replacing an indisposed Veronica Dunne, tenor James Johnston and violinists, Hungarian-born Francois D'Albert, who had come to live in Ireland in 1949 and then taught in the Royal Irish Academy of Music, and Jaroslav Vaneček.

To assist in publicising these concerts the services of Seymour Leslie, who had so successfully promoted the Adelaide Hospital events, were employed. The concerts and another three in March 1953 proved highly popular with very satisfactory attendances. My own first RÉSO 'Prom' concert was on 22 March that year, when an all Tchaikovsky programme with the Danish pianist, France Ellegaard, was conducted by Winfried Zillig of the Frankfurt Radio Orchestra. History repeated itself with applause after the first movement of the Concerto. Prices ranged from 2s.6d to 7s.6d [Today, £1.85-£5.65].

The DGOS Spring Season at the Gaiety in 1953 brought three productions from the repertoire of the State Opera in Munich. The RÉSO accompanied as it

Gaiety Theatre, Dublin

had done with the visits of the Hamburg company in 1950 and 1951. The Bavarian operas were *Tristan und Isolde,* conducted by legendary Robert Heger; *The Marriage of Figaro,* under the baton of Hans Gierster and *La Bohème,* directed by Karl Tutein.

On 29 September that year Aloys Fleischmann conducted a concert of music by Arnold Bax at the Phoenix Hall in the composer's presence. Harriet Cohen, the companion of Bax for many years, was the soloist in the Piano Concertante for the Left Hand - written for Miss Cohen when she injured her right hand in an accident, and of which Fleischmann had conducted the premiere on 17 October 1950. The other works this time were the tone poem of the Cúchulain legend 'The Garden of Fand' and the 'Overture to Adventure'. After the concert Bax visited Cork, a favourite spot of his, as Fleischmann's guest. He suffered a heart attack on 3 October in the Fleischmann home and died there that evening.

In less fraught circumstances the DGOS Winter Season of 1953 welcomed the return of the Hamburg State Opera with Leopold Ludwig conducting *Don Giovanni* and Heinz Walburg undertaking *The Abduction from the Seraglio.* The Orchestra was readily responsive.

The Orchestral roll-call for early 1953 showed a number of new names in several departments. Among the strings were Ettie Baigel, Yvonne Bizet, Doris Lawlor, Eileen Parfrey and David Lillis among the violins; Kathleen Green and Shirley Pollard in the violas; Thomas Kelly and Otto Pacholke, cellos, and Hans Engel in the double-basses. In the brass Diego Benedusi was among the trumpets and Ewald Werner, trombone. Val Keogh, for many years the Orchestra's indomitable Manager, was then in the percussion section.

This was also the year when it was decided to strengthen the string sections and employ extra brass and wood-wind forces rather than continue using ad hoc extras which the repertoire frequently demanded. While the RÉSO's strength now technically rose to seventy-two, it was not officially established at this level until 1958.

In order to achieve this objective, advertisements were placed in the Berlin papers. Fachtna Ó hAnnracháin and Milan Horvat travelled to Berlin to audition for suitable musicians and in this task they were assisted by members of the RIAS (Radio in the American Sector) Orchestra.

Among the chosen artists were tuba player Hartmut Pritzel who would be heard in the Vaughan Williams Concerto, and who remained the Orchestra's principal from December 1953 until his retirement in January 1997; trombonist Rudolf Jannasch who later went to Essen; bassoonist Dieter Prodöhl who, like oboe player Helmut Seeber, remained with the RÉSO until their respective retirements. The timpanist Kurt-Hans Goedike, then only eighteen and whose style, dash and handsome appearance made him something of a heart throb with the ladies of the audience, was another of these remarkable Berlin finds. He has long since been principal timpanist with the London Symphony Orchestra.

Gerard Meyer

Victor Malíř

Kurt-Hans Goedicke

Hartmut Pritzel

The audition also selected the violinists Max Thöner, who would lead the orchestra on a number of occasions, and Georg Gerike, who remained in Ireland until his death. The viola player Herbert Pöche was also part of this intake. He and Max Thöner would later (27 May 1955) be the soloists in Mozart's Sinfonia Concertante with Milan Horvat at the Phoenix Hall.

Separately to this a brilliant young Italian clarinettist, Michele Incenzo, came to the Orchestra in 1953. He led the section for a number of years and like other section leaders appeared as soloist with the orchestra on a number of occasions - the Mozart Concerto on 13 September 1957 under Carlo Franci, and Weber's Concertino on 18 September 1959 under Franco Patane. Incenzo's versatility, polish and élan are still remembered with affection by his colleagues and admirers.

1954 brought the French harpist Gerard Meyer to the Orchestra. He would be the soloist in both the Handel and Dittersdorf Concertos and would also marry RÉSO horn player, Ann Doyle. She was the daughter of JM and Nancy Doyle, who was then part of the RÉSO's cello line. In due course both left the orchestra to live and work in France where Gerard sadly died at a relatively early age. The flautist Hans Kohlmann also arrived in 1954. He too married an orchestral colleague, violinist Eileen Parfrey, and remained with the orchestra until his tragic death in a drowning accident in 1976.

The horn player Victor Mališ came to Ireland from Slovenia that year as well to become the section's principal, a position he held with distinction until illness forced him to step down in 1980. The Mozart, Richard Strauss and Hindemith Concertos allowed him to shine as soloist on several occasions. Mr Mališ, who married in Dublin many years ago, later became manager of the RTÉ Concert Orchestra, retiring in 1991. His daughter Andreja has been the Symphony Orchestra's harpist since 1988.

Regional Concerts

While Radio Éireann had not been involved in organising public concerts in Dublin off its own bat, between 1948 and 1953 the Orchestra had travelled to venues outside the capital. In order to facilitate the smooth running of these operations, Kevin Roche had been appointed the first Orchestra Manager in 1952. In April that year the Orchestra visited Tuam. The concert, in the Odeon Cinema, was conducted by JM Doyle and the soloist was soprano Joan Walker. The musicians of the RÉSO were met on arrival by 'the Chairman and members of the Town Board and a number of prominent citizens'. The attendance at the concert included the Archbishop of Tuam to whom 'members of the Orchestra were presented'.

Even before that, the RÉSO had visited Waterford on 25 January 1950 when at the Olympia Ballroom Francesco Mander conducted Beethoven's Fifth Symphony. The soloists were the Waterford-born singers Maura O'Connor and William Watt who were heard in arias by Weber and Coleridge-Taylor. The following morning brought a children's concert attended by two thousand young people. Under Milan Horvat it gave concerts in Belfast on 1 and 2 (for schools) February 1951 with tenor Walter Midgley as soloist.

Cork City Hall

A concert in Cork in January 1952 was highly successful, with Spanish pianist Gonzalo Soriano heard in Beethoven's Third Piano Concerto under the direction of Otto Matzerath.

The Orchestra also appeared in concert at the Wexford Festival (the Radio Éireann Light Orchestra accompanied the opera performances due to the minute size of Wexford's Theatre Royal pit) on 1 November 1952 - the second year of the festival's operation - when its soloist at the Abbey Cinema, under Milan Horvat, was the pianist Joseph Weingarten. The Symphony Orchestra eventually took over the opera performances in 1962 after the Theatre Royal had undergone a number of structural enhancements.

Touring continued and expanded into what is now a regular annual feature of its work. The Orchestra visited Northern Ireland again in October 1954 when under Milan Horvat and with Joseph Szigeti as soloist - employing a violinist avoided the difficulties of piano transportation and saved platform space - it travelled to Belfast and Derry. En route the Orchestra gave its first concert in Dundalk and returned via Sligo for its first appearance there. The concert programme of Beethoven's Violin Concerto and Tchaikovsky's Fourth Symphony was repeated in Dublin on the Orchestra's return.

February 1955 had concerts in Cork, Limerick and Waterford and there was a Northern return in September of that year. Then Newry, Belfast and Derry were visited before concerts in Sligo and Galway. Again this programme, under Horvat, was repeated at a Gaiety 'Prom'. In November 1957 the RÉSO crossed the border once more to appear with the Belfast Philharmonic Society as part of the first Belfast Festival.

Policy on Irish composers

In a bid to promote the work of Irish composers it was Fachtna Ó hAnnracháin's idea to include a short Irish work in each of the public concerts - a policy in fact inaugurated in the Bowles era and now revived and retained for many years. It was through another Ó hAnnracháin initiative that Radio Éireann's Carolan Prize, named after the celebrated blind harpist/composer Turlough Carolan (1670-1738), was offered on an annual basis from 1949/50. Valued at £100, it was presented for a work for full orchestra. The first winner was Havelock Nelson with his Sinfonietta, which received its premiere in the Phoenix Hall during March 1951, with the composer conducting.

The winner in 1951 was AJ Potter, with his combined 'Overture to a Kitchen Comedy' and 'Rhapsody under a High Sky' and again in 1952 with the Concerto da Chiesa, for piano and orchestra. The Overture and Rhapsody were heard for the first time on 17 June 1952 under Jean Meylan while Milan Horvat conducted the premiere of the Concerto with Anthony Hughes in the Phoenix Hall on 25 September 1953. Brian Boydell's Violin Concerto was the winning work in 1953. It was dedicated to Jaroslav Vaneček, then violin professor at the Municipal School of Music, who premiered the work under the composer's direction in the Phoenix Hall in October 1954. A performance of a slightly revised version was given by Vaneček under Milan

Valerie (left) and Joan Trimble

18 September 1953
Phoenix Hall

Handel: Concerto grosso in D minor
Mozart: Flute Concerto, K313
Martinů: Symphony no 4

André Prieur, flute
Milan Horvat, conductor

25 September 1953
Phoenix Hall

Bach: Brandenburg Concerto no 3
A J Potter: Piano Concerto*
Beethoven: Symphony no 3 ('Eroica')

Anthony Hughes, piano
Milan Horvat, conductor
**winner of Carolan Prize, 1952*
**First Performance*

25 October 1953
Gaiety Theatre

Weber: Overture, 'Euryanthe'
Chopin: Piano Concerto no 2
Larchet: Dirge of Ossian
Larchet: MacAnanty's Reel
Tchaikovsky: Symphony no 5

Charles Lynch, piano
Milan Horvat, conductor

1 November 1953
Gaiety Theatre

Vaughan Williams: Overture, 'The Wasps'
Beethoven: Violin Concerto
Schubert: Symphony no 8
Moeran: In the Mountain Country

Antonio Brosa, violin
Milan Horvat, conductor
This concert was repeated in Wexford, with Max Rostal as soloist

15 November 1953
Gaiety Theatre

Smetana: Overture, 'The Bartered Bride'
Duff : 'Drinking Horn' suite
Dvořák: Cello Concerto
Beethoven: Symphony no 5

Paul Tortelier, cello
Milan Horvat, conductor

24 January 1954
Gaiety Theatre

Beethoven: Overture, Leonora no 3
Mozart: Concerto for 2 pianos, K365
Brian Boydell: Suite, The Buried Moon
Dvořák: Eight Slavonic Dances

Joan and Valerie Trimble, pianos
Milan Horvat, conductor

Appointment of a principal conductor

Horvat in the Gaiety on 30 January 1955. Erskine Childers (later President) was now Minister for Posts and Telegraphs and Maurice Gorham had become Director of Radio Éireann in January 1953. Under the Minister's direction Comhairle Radio Éireann came into being, its purpose being 'broadly speaking' to take the place of the Department of Posts and Telegraphs in assisting the Minister in the framing of policy and carrying out the administration of broadcasting. Its five man membership included Charles J Brennan, then a young managing director of an insurance firm and noted for his wide ranging musical interests, and Patrick Lynch, subsequently Professor of Economics in University College, Dublin, and who later became Chairman of the national airline, Aer Lingus.

Childers was not naturally inclined to an interest in music, but recognised that 'a symphony orchestra was the apex of culture in any country', and he wanted to make the RÉSO 'at least as good as the Hallé'. (Over the previous five years, the cost of the Orchestra had risen from £55 - to £66,000 - £220-264,000 in today's money - plus another £5,000 [£20,000] to meet the costs of public concerts and tours). He later said that, as his duties required him to attend concerts in an official capacity, he had developed a love of the symphonic repertoire. As President of Ireland he was an assiduous attender of the RTÉSO concerts, not only at the Gaiety Theatre but also at the Saint Francis Xavier Hall - a trend followed by his successor, Cearbhaill Ó Dalaigh.

However, one possible accession of a cadre of German players was resisted by the Comhairle - in 1953 nineteen members of the Prussia State Orchestra expressed their interest in escaping from East Berlin and settling in Ireland, but the view was taken that only ten could be accommodated, and this new contingent began to enter the Orchestra's ranks in the following year.

This was also the period when Cork asserted its demand for a resident orchestra, which it wanted supplied by Radio Éireann. The debate was waged heatedly, chiefly by the redoutable Aloys Fleischmann, and, rather predictably, resisted by RÉ. However, a successful compromise was reached in that RÉ, sensing that it did indeed have a responsibility to provide live music for the citizens of the southern capital, offered the services of a resident string quartet, and since 1956 the successive RÉ and later RTÉ String Quartets (at present the Vanbrugh) have constituted an invaluable resource for the public and for students of music through their association with University College and the Cork School of Music - and representing the only quartet in the world to be maintained in residence by a broadcasting station. A second successful outcome of Cork's campaign for an orchestra was the extension of a number of RÉSO concerts each year to the City Hall in Cork, which has proved a fine venue acoustically.

The idea of appointing a principal conductor also arose around 1952-53. Milan Horvat (b 1919), already well tried on the RÉSO rostrum, was offered a three-year contract. His appointment had been agreed at a preliminary meeting of Comhairle Radio Éireann in early 1953. He accepted, becoming the orchestra's first Principal Conductor in August 1953, but news of his appointment had been

17 January 1954
Gaiety Theatre

Mozart: Symphony no 41, K551
Mozart: Horn Concerto no 4, K495
Fleischmann: Suite, An Cóitín Dearg
Richard Strauss: Horn Concerto no 1
Rimsky-Korsakov: Capriccio Espagnol

Dennis Brain, horn
Milan Horvat, conductor

17 October 1954
Gaiety Theatre

Rossini: Overture, 'The Thieving Magpie'
Harty: Fair Day from 'Irish Symphony'
Beethoven: Violin Concerto
Tchaikovsky: Symphony no 4

Joseph Szigeti, violin
Milan Horvat, conductor
This programme was also performed in Dundalk, Sligo and, on the Orchestra's first visit to Northern Ireland, in Derry, and Belfast

7 November 1954
Gaiety Theatre

Rezniček: Overture, 'Donna Diana'
Cimarosa: Oboe Concerto
Beethoven: Symphony no 1
Walter Beckett: Triple fantasy from Suite for Orchestra*
Richard Strauss: Oboe Concerto
Rossini: Overture, 'William Tell'

Léon Goossens, oboe
Milan Horvat, conductor
**First performance*

9 January 1955
Gaiety Theatre

Prokofiev: Symphony no 1 ('Classical')
Ina Boyle: Wild Geese
Tchaikovsky: Violin Concerto
Debussy: La Mer
Wagner: Overture, 'Die Meistersinger'

Henry Holst, violin
Milan Horvat, conductor

16 January 1955
Gaiety Theatre

Vivaldi: Concerto Grosso in G minor
Harty: John Field Suite
Schumann: Cello Concerto
Beethoven: Symphony no 3 ('Eroica')

André Navarra, cello
Milan Horvat, conductor

23 January 1955
Gaiety Theatre

Weber: Overture, 'Der Freischütz'
Victory: 'Elegy' and 'Marche Pittoresque'
Liszt: Piano Concerto no 1
Schubert: Symphony no 9

Ginette Doyen, piano
Milan Horvat, conductor

6 February 1955
Gaiety Theatre

Bach/Respighi: Prelude & Fugue in D
Beethoven: Piano Concerto no 5 ('Emperor')
A J Potter: Variations on a popular tune*
Dvořák: Symphony no 9

Anthony Hughes, piano
Milan Horvat, conductor
**First performance*

4 March 1955
Phoenix Hall

Holst: 'The Perfect Fool'
Bax: Tintagel
Elgar: Enigma Variations
Walton: Symphony no 1

George Weldon, conductor

kept secret for political reasons for some months. (As with most other Eastern European countries under communist régimes at the time, official relations between Ireland and Yugoslavia were cold.) The contract stipulated that Horvat would be available to the RÉSO for eight months each year but was also free to undertake other engagements at home and abroad (one of which would be with the Berlin Philharmonic Orchestra). Radio Éireann would still have openings for guest conductors as well.

The Horvat years

Milan Horvat's term of office proved highly successful and his contract was renewed for 1956/57 and again for the 1957/58 season. As time went on he had his critics but this was probably inevitable for anyone who would be involved with so many concerts over a relatively short period of time, and, as Maurice Gorham observed, 'that is the fate that threatens any permanent conductor in the small world that is known as "Dublin musical circles"'. Horvat's programmes were firmly rooted in the classical and romantic repertoires but contemporary music, particularly new works by Irish composers, also found their way into his concerts. Indeed JJ O'Reilly's 'Remembrance - Nocturne for Milan Horvat' was dedicated to the conductor as a tribute to his commitment to the cause of Irish composers during his term of office with Radio Éireann. Horvat premiered the piece in the Gaiety on 16 February 1958 which was his last 'Prom' concert as Principal Conductor.

Other Irish works during Horvat's tenure included JJ O'Reilly's tone poem 'Oluf' which had its premiere at the Abbey Lecture Hall in October 1954, the Phoenix Hall being out of action, while a Piano Concerto by Gerard Victory, a man who would have a very prominent role in music in Radio Éireann in the coming years, had its first performance by Anthony Hughes under Horvat's baton on 8 November, also at the Abbey Lecture Hall.

A memorial to Sibelius, who died on 20 September 1957, included 'Finlandia', 'Pohjola's Daughter' and the Fourth Symphony in a programme conducted by JM Doyle on 15 November. The first performance of Seoirse Bodley's *'Salve, Maria Virgo'* took place at a Gaiety 'Prom' on 27 October. The work had been commissioned by the Franciscan Friars of Dublin's Adam and Eve's Church to celebrate the tercentenary of Father Luke Wadding, a theologian deeply involved with promoting the cause of the Immaculate Conception.

Towards the end of his term, in February 1958, Horvat had directed a performance of Bartók's Second Piano Concerto with Edith Farnadi on 2nd. This was coupled with the premiere of AJ Potter's 'Finnegan's Wake' which, like the first movement of the Bartók, was scored for woodwind, brass and percussion. Milan Horvat continued with the orchestra until the summer. He conducted the Webern Passacaglia and Britten Violin Concerto with Jaroslav Vaneček on 27 June and Mozart's Piano Concerto in C, K 467 with Patricia Herbert on 4 July 1958. His valedictory work was Bruckner's Ninth, and last, Symphony.

Milan Horvat continued to make a number of guest appearances with the

11 March 1955
Phoenix Hall

Dvořák: The Water Sprite
Wagner: Siegfried Idyll
Ian Whyte: Scots Suite
Beethoven: Overture, 'Prometheus'
Sibelius: Symphony no 1

Ian Whyte, conductor

27 May 1955
Phoenix Hall

Cherubini: Symphony in D
Franck: Symphonic variations
Falla: Dances from 'The Three Cornered Hat'
Liadov: The Enchanted Lake
Richard Strauss: Tod und Verklärung

Anthony Hughes, piano
Francesco Mander, conductor

3 June 1955
Phoenix Hall

Bach: Brandenburg Concerto no 6
Mozart: Sinfonia Concertante, K364
Hindemith: Mathis der Maler

Max Thöner, violin
Herbert Pöche, viola
Milan Horvat, conductor

29 July 1955
Metropolitan Hall

Dvořák: Symphonic Variations
Bliss: Piano Concerto*
Sibelius: Symphony no 5

Charles Lynch, piano
J M Doyle, conductor
**First Irish performance*

30 October 1955
Olympia Theatre

Rossini: Overture, 'The Barber of Seville'
T C Kelly: Three Pieces for Strings
Beethoven: Piano Concerto no 4
Mendelssohn: Symphony no 4
Kodály: Dances of Galanta

Cor de Groot, piano
Milan Horvat, conductor

6 November 1955
Olympia Theatre

Weber: Overture, 'Euryanthe'
A J Potter: Rhapsody under a High Sky
Schumann: Piano Concerto
Brahms: Symphony no 1

Charles Lynch, piano
Eimear Ó Broin, conductor

8 November 1955
Abbey Lecture Hall

Reger: Mozart Variations
Victory: Piano Concerto*

Anthony Hughes, piano
Milan Horvat, conductor
**First performance*

20 November 1955
Olympia Theatre

Brahms: Academic Festival Overture
Brahms: Piano Concerto no 1
Tchaikovsky: Symphony no 6 ('Pathétique')

Shura Cherkassky, piano
Milan Horvat, conductor

RÉSO until 1962. Indeed his only appearance in the Gaiety pit was in the DGOS Winter Season of 1958 when he conducted a number of performances of *La Bohème* with Renato Cioni as Rodolfo. Concerts in May 1959 had Geraldine O'Grady, Gilbert Berg and János Fürst, a Hungarian violinist who, with a number of compatriots, had joined the orchestra following the 1956 uprising, as his soloists.

Horvat's programme on 22 May included Shostakovich's Tenth Symphony and this was also the mainstay of his final Dublin concert in the Phoenix Hall on 20 January 1962.

Following Horvat's departure as Principal Conductor the latter half of 1958 and most of 1959 were marked by a number of visiting English conductors among them Maurice Miles, Bryan Balkwill, Lawrence Leonard, Gerald Gentry and Vilem Tausky. Balkwill, indeed, was one of the DGOS conductors in the Winter Season of 1958. He took charge of four performances of *Don Giovanni* (24, 26, 28 November and 1 December) when Geraint Evans sang the title role with Martin Lawrence as Leporello. The Donna Anna to Dermot Troy's Don Ottavio was none other than Joan Sutherland and the opera was produced by Anthony Besch.

Appointment of an assistant conductor

In June 1953 a selection board had been set up to recommend the appointment of an assistant conductor for the RÉSO. Two young Dublin musicians, Sydney Bryans and Eimear Ó Broin, had recently come to the fore. They shared conducting duties until 1955 when Ó Broin became assistant to Milan Horvat. Eimear Ó Broin was a graduate of University College, Dublin, and had attended the Summer Schools in Dublin from 1946.

In 1950 he entered the Paris Conservatoire where he studied under Eugene Bigot who also conducted the Lamoureux and French Radio Orchestras. Besides his conducting classes, in which he was awarded a *premier prix* in 1952, Ó Broin attended the courses of Olivier Messiaen and Nadia Boulanger. After his highly successful Parisian studies Eimear Ó Broin spent a further year studying in Munich.

His first concert with the RÉSO was on 26 August 1952 when his programme was devoted to Beethoven's *Coriolanus* Overture and Eighth Symphony and Debussy's 'La Mer'. Following his return from Munich in June 1953 a programme consisted of Arthur Duff's Irish Suite for Strings and Schumann's Fourth Symphony. From then on until his retirement from RTÉ in 1989 Eimear Ó Broin conducted a vast repertoire with both the Symphony and Light (later Concert,) Orchestras and conducted and introduced very many of Ceol-chumann na nÓg's concerts.

His programmes included the premieres of many Irish works and the introduction of innumerable compositions to Irish audiences for the first time. These included a memorable performance of Hindemith's *Die Harmonie der Welt* Symphony on 31 July 1959 just under two years following the Munich premiere of the opera from which Hindemith arranged the work. Ó Broin's

12 February 1956
Gaiety Theatre

Mozart:	Serenata notturna K 239
Brian Boydell:	Megalithic Ritual Dances*
Ravel:	Piano Concerto
Franck:	Symphony in D

Monique Haas, piano
Milan Horvat, conductor
**First performance, RTÉ commission*

27 January 1957
Gaiety Theatre

Brahms:	Tragic Overture
Larchet:	By the Waters of Moyle
Beethoven:	Violin Concerto
Borodin:	Symphony no 2

Jean Fournier, violin
Milan Horvat, conductor

3 February 1957
Gaiety Theatre

Wagner:	Overture, 'The Flying Dutchman'
May:	Lyric Movement
Bartók:	Piano Concerto no 3
Beethoven:	Symphony no 3 ('Eroica')

Edith Farnadi, piano
Milan Horvat, conductor

15 March 1957
Phoenix Hall

Bach:	Brandenburg Concerto no 3
Mozart:	Concerto for two pianos, K365
Mozart:	Overture, 'La Clemenza di Tito'
Prokofiev:	Symphony no 5

Patricia and Nuala Herbert, pianos
Milan Horvat, conductor

29 March 1957
Phoenix Hall

Shostakovich:	Symphony no 10*
Schubert:	Symphony no 3

Milan Horvat, conductor
**First Irish performance*

5 April 1957
Phoenix Hall

Rossini:	Overture, 'La Cenerentola'
Franci:	Music for Strings and Timpani*
Beethoven:	Symphony no 2
Mussorgsky/ Ravel:	Pictures at an Exhibition

Carlo Franci, conductor
**First Irish performance*

Elgar centenary

31 May 1957 Phoenix Hall	9 June 1957 Theatre Royal
Symphony no 2	The Dream of Gerontius
Bach/Elgar: Fantasia and Fugue in C minor	Constance Shacklock, contralto
Introduction and Allegro	Ronald Dowd, tenor
	Marian Nowakowski, bass
Overture, Cockaigne	Our Lady's Choral Society
J M Doyle, conductor	Sir John Barbirolli, conductor

5 July 1957
Phoenix Hall

Papandopulou:	Amphitryon Suite
Wagner:	Siegfried Idyll
Mahler:	Kindertotenlieder
Rachmaninov:	Symphony no 2

Austin Gaffney, baritone
Milan Horvat, conductor

engagements abroad took him to Belgium, Britain, Denmark, Finland, France, Germany, the Netherlands and Italy.

A young pianist who would soon become very active in Ireland's music making, Veronica McSwiney, made her début with the Orchestra on 11 September when she played Dohnanyi's Nursery Song Variations under the baton of Franco Patane.

An unusual event took place in June 1959 with two Barbirolli concerts promoted by the Dublin International Festival of Music and the Arts which had the famous conductor as its patron. The first of these, at the Gaiety, had the formidable Gina Bachauer in the Brahms Second Piano Concerto, while the second concert at the Theatre Royal found the RÉSO making minor history when it joined forces with Manchester's Hallé Orchestra, of which Barbirolli was conductor, for the first performance in Ireland of Mahler's 'Resurrection' Symphony. The Orchestras were led by Martin Milner of the Hallé and the soloists with Our Lady's Choral Society were Victoria Elliott and Eugenia Zareska. It was a thrilling occasion.

The Italian Carlo Franci, who had given a number of concerts with the Orchestra, had become quite friendly with John Reidy (Seán Ó Riada) who followed Arthur Duff as Assistant Director of Music from 1953 to 1956. It was he who gave the first performance of Reidy's *'Hercules Dux Ferrariae'* on 13 September 1957. He was considered a likely candidate to succeed Horvat as Principal Conductor. Indeed he was almost offered the post until difficulties arose and negotiations with Signor Franci were discontinued. Matters were left in abeyance with the RÉSO's register of visiting guest conductors continuing for the time being. Among those who filled the gaps left open by the non-appointment of Franci were the English musicians Lawrence Leonard and Maurice Miles, Francesco Mander, JM Doyle and Eimear Ó Broin.

Début of Tibor Paul

Maurice Gorham had been approached by the director of the Australian Broadcasting Corporation, Charles Moses, with the suggestion of, if possible, engaging the Hungarian conductor, Tibor Paul, who had considerable experience in the southern hemisphere, to conduct some concerts during Paul's visit to Europe in the autumn of 1958. While Radio Éireann's initial response was negative, because of prior commitments, Tibor Paul, a man of undoubted talent but prone to self-aggrandizement, was in fact engaged for a concert in November that year in a slot left vacant by Signor Franci. He was appointed Principal Conductor from 1961on a contractual basis. There were some positive and some negative aspects to his tenure of office.

Changes in the structure of Radio Éireann

The 1960s brought a period of change to Radio Éireann. The Broadcasting Authority Act was passed by Dáil Éireann on 6 April 1960 and one month later the Radio Éireann Authority came into being. It was headed by Éamon Andrews and among the nine-member body were Ernest Blythe of the Abbey Theatre (and a former Minister for Finance) and

12 July 1957
Phoenix Hall

Mendelssohn: Overture, 'A Midsummer Night's Dream'
Ravel: Pavane for a Dead Infanta
Françaix: Piano Concertino
Honegger: Symphony no 5
Ó Riada: The Banks of Sullane*
Turina: Rhapsodia Sinfonica

Patricia Herbert, piano
Eimear Ó Broin, conductor
**First performance*

27 October 1957
Gaiety Theatre

Cimarosa: Overture, 'The Secret Marriage'
Seoirse Bodley: 'Salve Maria Virgo'*
Glazunov: Violin Concerto
Bruckner: Symphony no 4

Margaret Hayes, violin
Milan Horvat, conductor
**First performance*

14 November 1958
Phoenix Hall

Verdi: Overture, 'La Forza del Destino'
Richard Strauss: Don Juan
Delius: Prelude, 'Irmelin'
Boris Blacher: Paganini Variations*
Beethoven: Symphony no 7

Tibor Paul, conductor
**First Irish performance*
This was Tibor Paul's first concert with the RTÉSO. Reaction was favourable, and Paul was invited to return the following autumn for a series of concerts:

22 September 1959
Phoenix Hall

Douglas: Essay for Strings
Respighi: Fountains of Rome
Mozart: Symphony no 41, K551

25 September 1959
Phoenix Hall

Rossini: Overture, 'The Barber of Seville'
Flothuis: Symphonic Music
Kodály: Háry János Suite
Dvořák: Symphony no 9

2 October 1959
Phoenix Hall

Theodore Karyotakis: Suite for Orchestra
Richard Strauss: Also Sprach Zarathustra
Beethoven: Symphony no 5

6 October 1959
Phoenix Hall

Bartók: Divertimento
Barraud: Symphony no 3

18 October 1959
Gaiety Theatre

Wagner: Overture, 'Tannhäuser'
Brian Boydell: In Memoriam Mahatma Gandhi
Rachmaninov: Piano Concerto no 3
Brahms: Symphony no 2

Monique de la Bouchollerie, piano

25 October 1959
Gaiety Theatre

Handel: Concerto Grosso in G minor
May: Sunlight and Shadow
Mendelssohn: Violin Concerto
Tchaikovsky: Symphony no 6 ('Pathétique')

Ralph Holmes, violin

24 January 1960
Gaiety Theatre

Duff: Irish Suite for strings
Mozart: Piano Concerto no 24, K491
Mahler: Symphony no 5

Louis Kentner, piano
Tibor Paul, conductor

Charles Brennan from the defunct Comhairle Radio Éireann.

The Authority took over 380 staff from the Department of Posts and Telegraphs with the musicians from both Radio Éireann Orchestras making up a significant percentage of the transferred personnel. As the musicians moved so did a variety of musical instruments including sixteen pianos, seven of them concert grands, a vast quantity of scores, gramophone records and copyrights. The two halls outside the GPO - the Phoenix and the one at Portobello which housed the Light Orchestra - also came under the Authority's control.

In November 1960 the Authority appointed American Edward J Roth, Junior, as the first Director-General of Radio Éireann/Telefís Éireann (the two names were later amalgamated to form Radio Telefís Éireann). He had been a management consultant with NBC in the United States and had the experience of establishing television stations in Mexico and Peru. He was engaged for a period of two years and while he became increasingly interested in sound broadcasting, his main concern was obviously to start the Irish television service. The contract for the television studios at Montrose in Donnybrook had already been signed in October 1960 and as the development towards television continued, personnel were gradually moved to it.

Observing the scene as it was unfolding, Fachtna Ó hAnnracháin asked to be allowed to relinquish his post of Director of Music. His request was granted and he became Legal and Contracts Officer to the Authority. A panel, which included William Glock of the BBC, was set up to find a suitable replacement, and the Cork-born, Dublin-educated and BBC Belfast-based Havelock Nelson was invited to become Radio Éireann's Director of Music. However after some deliberation Nelson, settled, well-known and highly respected in Northern Ireland, decided against a return to Dublin and declined the Radio Éireann post.

The spotlight now turned to Tibor Paul who, having indicated his desire to see the jobs of Principal Conductor and Music Director again merged into one, was invited by Edward Roth to assume the additional post. This he readily accepted. The decision would lead to Paul's ultimate downfall and eventual removal from the Irish music scene.

When Renzo Marchionni left the RÉSO to return to Italy in 1959 the leader's position was left vacant for some time but towards the end of that year it was filled for three months by John Ronayne. In March 1960 Mr Ronayne departed again and Geraldine O'Grady, following the tradition of Terry O'Connor and Nancie Lord, took over the leader's chair. Her first Phoenix Hall concert on 18 March was conducted by Lawrence Leonard, her second by Ottavio Ziino whose own Second Symphony was on the programme.

Tibor Paul - his first two years

Tibor Paul was a graduate of the Royal Academy of Music in Budapest. One of his teachers was Kodály, another Felix Weingartner. He began his conducting career in 1937 and obtained a succession of important appointments in his native

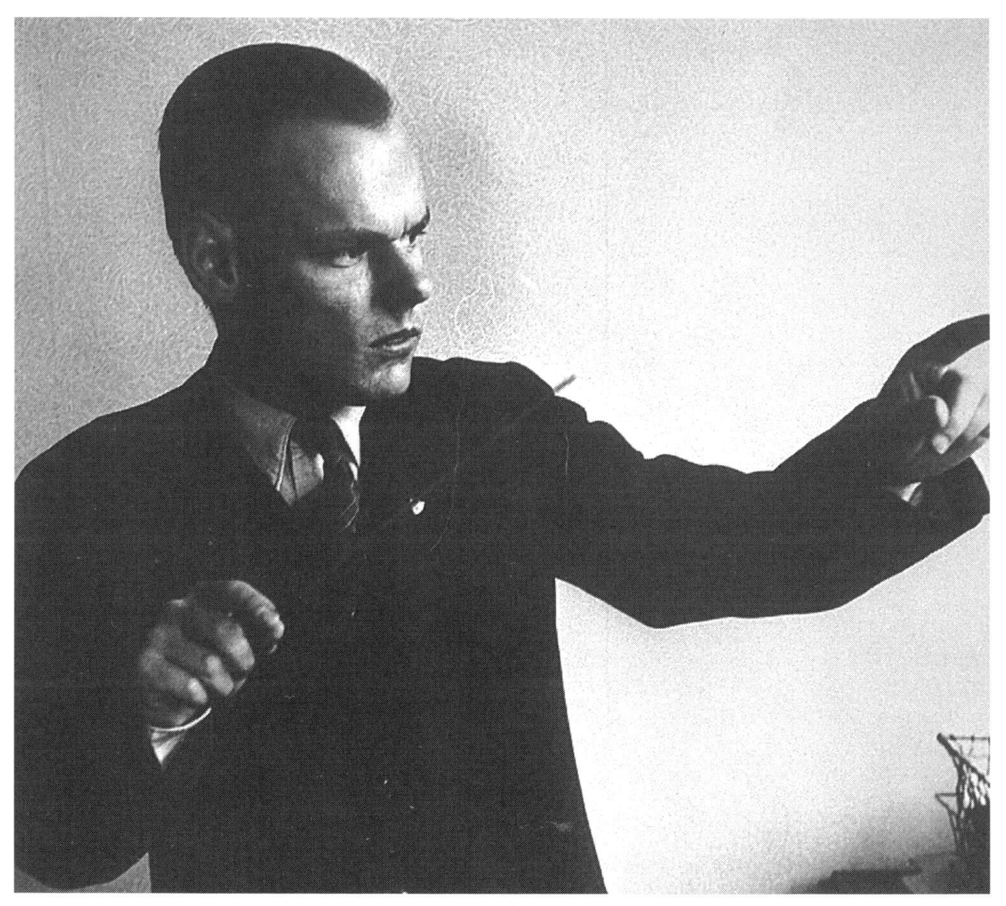

Eimear Ó Broin

In 1957 as part of a programme for advancing the careers of young conductors devised by the London Philharmonic Orchestra, Eimear Ó Broin shared the highest award with Colin Davis. As a result he conducted the LPO in a concert of Rossini, Tchaikovsky, Haydn (Trumpet Concerto with Eric Bravington) and Beethoven (Seventh Symphony). In the following year - 1958 - two of Eimear Ó Broin's Phoenix Hall concerts were broadcast directly by the BBC which had been intrigued by the remarkable repertoire which was being regularly relayed by Radio Éireann. His programmes included May's 'Songs from Prison', Duff's 'Echoes of Georgian Dublin', Debussy's 'La Mer' and Bax's 'Tintagel'. He has also distinguished himself as a musicologist.

country and in Switzerland. He moved to Australia where he made his home in 1953 on being appointed conductor of the National Opera in Sydney and Professor of Conducting in the New South Wales Conservatory.

While Tibor Paul was not actually appointed Principal Conductor until late 1961 his engagements with the RÉSO became more numerous from the beginning of 1960. One of his earliest concerts that year was in the Theatre Royal on 15 January with the celebrated violinist Gioconda de Vito as soloist in the Brahms Concerto. Paul's symphony was Beethoven's Fifth and the evening opened with AJ Potter's ballet music *Careless Love* which had been premiered the previous year.

This in fact was the launching pad of Concert and Assembly Halls Limited, a subsidiary of the Music Association of Ireland set up initially as a sub committee of the Association's Council as early as 1951 with the specific aim of establishing a national concert hall in Dublin. Among the leading lights on this project almost ten years later were Olive Smith, lawyer/composer Edgar Deale, architect Michael Scott and Guinness magnate Lord Moyne. Tibor Paul was an enthusiastic supporter.

In other notable concerts during 1960 Hungarian János Fürst, then in the violin ranks but who would leave the orchestra and eventually return as Principal Conductor, was the soloist in the Kabalevsky Concerto on 26 February. Baritone Austin Gaffney, later to have tremendous success in the world of operetta, undertook Mahler's *Kindertotenlieder* on 11 March. Under Sydney Bryans, Stravinsky's Symphony in Three Movements proved an excellent foil.

Mahler's *Lieder eines fahrenden Gesellen* was featured on 10 June when the soloist was the young alto Bernadette Greevy, whose celebrated career continues undiminished. Her conductor was the distinguished Walter Goehr, father of composer Alexander Goehr, who haloed the Mahler with the Fifth Symphonies of Schubert and Martinů. This Czech composer's Violin Concerto was played by Margaret Hayes in the Phoenix Hall on 15 July with Jean Meylan conducting. Later Miss Hayes spent many years with the Philharmonia Orchestra in London before returning again to live and teach in Dublin.

Among other visiting conductors were Vilem Tausky, Milan Horvat, Lawrence Leonard, Maurice Miles and Hans Mueller-Kray who directed the premiere of Seoirse Bodley's First Symphony at the Gaiety on 23 October. Franco Patane, who had been part of the DGOS Spring Season, introduced Franco Alfano's ballet score *Eliana* at the Phoenix Hall on 27 May.

As part of the Dublin Festival of Music and the Arts, which now had John Barbirolli as President, at the Theatre Royal on 30 June Constantin Silvestri conducted Bodley's *'Salve, Maria Virgo'*, Dvořák's 'New World' Symphony and Beethoven's Violin Concerto with Isaac Stern. During the work a string snapped on Stern's instrument; undeterred he took over Arthur Nachstern's fiddle and continued unabashed.
Paul's first concert of 1961 was on 3 January. Programming Liszt's 'Totentanz'

31 January 1960
Gaiety Theatre

Wagner: Overture, 'The Flying Dutchman'
Stanford: Irish Rhapsody no 1
Bruch: Violin Concerto no 1
Tchaikovsky: Symphony no 4

Geraldine O'Grady, violin
Maurice Miles, conductor

16 September 1960
Phoenix Hall

Mozart programme:

Divertimento, K334
Oboe Concerto, K314
Symphony no 39, K549

Ian Wilson, oboe
Tibor Paul, conductor

23 September 1960
Phoenix Hall

Beethoven: Overture, 'Egmont'
Beethoven: Symphony no 6 ('Pastoral')
Richard Strauss: Don Quixote

Maurice Meulien, cello
Tibor Paul, conductor

4 October 1960
Phoenix Hall

Mendelssohn: Symphony no 4
Hindemith: Mathis der Maler

Tibor Paul, conductor

6 November 1960
Gaiety Theatre

Debussy: Three Nocturnes
A J Potter: Cardinal Fleury Suite
Saint-Saëns: Cello Concerto no 1
Berlioz: Symphonie fantastique

János Starker, cello
Radio Éireann Singers (ladies' voices)
Tibor Paul, conductor

30 December 1960
Phoenix Hall

Messiaen: L'Ascension
Martinů: Oboe Concerto

Evelyn Rothwell, oboe
Tibor Paul, conductor

15 September 1961
Phoenix Hall

Bach: Orchestral Suite no 3
Bach: Brandenburg Concerto no 4
Dittersdorf: Symphony in C
Haydn: Symphony no 82 ('The Bear')

Geraldine O'Grady, violin,
André Prieur, Hans Kohlmann, flutes
Tibor Paul, conductor

1 October 1961
Olympia Theatre

Mozart: Symphony no 41, K551
Mahler: Kindertotenlieder
Richard Strauss: Ein Heldenleben

Aafje Heynis, contralto
Tibor Paul, conductor
Promoted by Concert and Assembly Halls Ltd

15 October 1961
Gaiety Theatre

Rimsky-Korsakov: Russian Easter Festival Overture
Fleischmann: Caoineadh Eilís Nic Dhiarmada Rua
Liszt: Piano Concerto no 2
Tchaikovsky: Symphony no 4

John Ogdon, piano
Tibor Paul, conductor

22 October 1961
Gaiety Theatre

Beethoven: Piano Concerto no 5 ('Emperor')
Bruckner: Symphony no 7

Kendall Taylor, piano
Tibor Paul, conductor

(Charles Lynch) may have been prophetic. In Paul's favour it must be said he gave the Orchestra a wider public image than it heretofore enjoyed and he had a sense of programming works which would have a broad public appeal. This is not to convey, however, that he abandoned the novel or unusual, as a look at his programmes over the coming years will show.

Still, his first major exposure in 1961 was in a Beethoven Festival in March at the Olympia Theatre which was part and parcel of Concert and Assembly Halls promotion in association with Radio Éireann. The five Piano Concertos and the Violin Concerto with the nine Symphonies were heard between 13 and 25 March. The pianists were Fou T'song, Anthony Hughes, Charles Lynch and Shura Cherkassky, who played both the Fourth and Fifth Concertos. Tibor Varga was the violinist with Veronica Dunne, Helen Watts, James Johnston and Roger Stalman undertaking the Ninth Symphony. The choral forces came from Radio Éireann's own groups. The festival was a phenomenal success with long queues each evening for the Olympia gallery.

The Dublin Festival of Music and the Arts in 1961 brought the welcome return of conductors Hans Schmidt-Isserstedt and Constantin Silvestri. Their concerts scheduled for the Theatre Royal had to be switched at the eleventh hour to the less salubrious ambiance of the National Stadium due to an industrial dispute outside the control of the organisers. Schmidt-Isserstedt had the young English pianist John Ogdon as his soloist in Liszt's First Concerto while Silvestri accompanied French cellist Pierre Fournier in the Dvořák Concerto. Irish music featured in both concerts with Arthur Duff's 'Hunting Horn Suite' in one and TC Kelly's 'Three Pieces' in the other.

Introduction of Subscription concerts

The following year, 1962, was no less interesting and developmental; indeed television had come to Ireland with Telefís Éireann transmitting for the first time on New Year's Eve 1961. The Orchestra's Gaiety events dropped the really unsuitable 'Prom' from their description in favour of the more acceptable 'Subscription' Concerts. These gave an opportunity to music lovers to indicate their commitment to the Orchestra by subscribing to a complete series of concerts. Up to the transfer from the Gaiety Theatre to the National Concert Hall, these traditionally consisted of five concerts during October and November and seven during the January-March period. They succeeded in attracting a capacity Sunday-night audience for almost their entire history.

The Concert Hall Fund figured in four April concerts in the Olympia. Paul decided on dedicated composers - Tchaikovsky, Wagner, Brahms and Bach - for each evening. His soloists were Abbey Simon, piano, Elsa Cavelti, soprano and Julius Katchen, piano in the first three with RTÉ's own choral forces being joined by the Culwick and Olivian Singers for Bach's B minor Mass in the fourth. The solos here were taken by Lucilla Indrigo, whose husband Dario was then among the RÉSO's violins, Bernadette Greevy, Dermot Troy and James Shaw.

Tibor Paul

At the Autumn 'Subscriptions' Paul took a bold step by celebrating Stravinsky's eightieth birthday with the first Irish performance of *The Rite of Spring* on 30 September at the Gaiety. He repeated the piece in Cork the following evening and two weeks later directed the first Irish performance of Kodály's *Psalmus Hungaricus* with the Dutch tenor Naan Pöld, the St James's Gate Choral Society and the O'Connell Schools Boys Choir. Paul's fondness for Kodály had already brought the composer's Symphony to the Phoenix Hall on 6 June.

Around this time a number of factors vied against the Phoenix Hall, one of which was Paul's desire to have a larger venue for his studio concerts. On 11 September 1962 he tried out the Jesuit-owned St Francis Xavier Hall in Upper Sherrard Street, adjacent to the Order's church in Upper Gardiner Street. Our Lady's Choral Society joined the orchestra for Mendelssohn's *Elijah*. Veronica Dunne, Lucilla Indrigo, Bernadette Greevy, Adrian de Peyer, Harvey Alan and treble Eugene Cranley were the soloists. The death knell for the Phoenix Hall, which also needed reconstruction work, had tolled.

Another venerable venue passed out of music's sphere when the Theatre Royal was demolished for redevelopment. However this was not before Our Lady's Choral Society gave a performance of the Berlioz *Requiem* there under Louis Frémaux on 23 March with soloist Ronald Dowd. It was a fitting valediction.

Elsewhere during 1962 the Italian conductor Napoleone Annovazzi who would, in due course, have a very lengthy association with the Dublin Grand Opera Society, and thereby the RÉSO, conducted two Phoenix Hall concerts in May. That on 22 May was devoted to Shostakovich's Tenth Symphony, the second time the work had been heard there in four months as Milan Horvat had included it in his 30 January programme.

In October a section of the Orchestra travelled to Wexford to accompany the performances of the Festival Opera. This task had been undertaken by the Radio Éireann Light Orchestra from the first Festival in 1951 until 1959. The following year found the event in recession as the town's Theatre Royal was completely renovated and its pit enlarged to accommodate about forty-five musicians. In 1961 the Liverpool Philharmonic Orchestra was engaged as the Festival's resident band, but from 1962 onwards the RÉSO has fulfilled this significant assignment with considerable acumen. Recently, its involvement with Wexford has given rise to a remarkable series of opera recordings for Naxos.

The Orchestra's first opera was Mascagni's *L'Amico Fritz,* conducted by Antonio Tonini and with Nicola Monti in the cast. The other opera that year, conducted by Gunnar Staern, was Bellini's *I Puritani,* with the young Mirella Freni as the lovelorn Elvira. As it was my own first Wexford production it retains a place of special affection for me. Despite the prestige which the Wexford Festival was attaching to itself it now seems odd that Tibor Paul conducted none of its productions. His position with Radio Éireann would surely have allowed him to more or less pick and choose what he wanted.

29 October 1961
Gaiety Theatre

Rossini: Overture, 'The Thieving Magpie'
Mendelssohn: Symphony no 4
A J Potter: 'Careless Love'
Ghedini: Sonata da Concerto
Liszt: Les Préludes

André Prieur, flute
Arthur Fiedler, conductor

17 February 1961
Phoenix Hall

J C Bach: Sinfonia no 3*
Telemann: Viola Concerto*
Khachaturian: 'Gayaneh' suite no 1*
Haydn: Symphony no 44 ('Trauer')
Holst: The Perfect Fool

Archie Collins, viola
Eimear Ó Broin* and Fred O'Callaghan, conductors

26 May 1961
Phoenix Hall

Vaughan Williams: Symphony no 6
Boccherini: Cello Concerto in B flat
Elgar: Falstaff

Coral Bognuda, cello
Maurice Miles, conductor

2 June 1961
Phoenix Hall

Beethoven: Overture, 'Prometheus'
Butterworth: Three Nocturnes
Chausson: Poème
Brahms: 'St Anthony' Variations
Walton: Symphony no 2*

Geraldine O'Grady, violin
Maurice Miles, conductor
**First Irish performance*

23 June 1961
Metropolitan Hall

Mendelssohn: Overture, 'Fingal's Cave'
Mozart: Violin Concerto in D K.ANH 249a
Richard Strauss: Suite, 'Le bourgeois gentilhomme'
Britten: Sinfonia da Requiem
Alwyn: Elizabethan Dances

Sheila O'Grady, violin
Bryan Balkwill, conductor

5 November 1961
Gaiety Theatre

Sibelius: Symphony no 7
Mendelssohn: Violin Concerto
Falla: Suite no 2, 'The Three Cornered Hat'
A J Potter: Rhapsody under a High Sky
Britten: Variations and Fugue on a theme of Purcell

Mary Gallagher, violin
Bryan Balkwill, conductor

2 March 1962
Phoenix Hall

Tchaikovsky: Serenade for strings
Berg: Violin Concerto*
Brahms: 'St Anthony' Variations
Debussy: Nocturnes - 'Nuages', 'Fetes'

Michel Chauveton, violin
Edgar Cosma, conductor
**First Irish performance*

23 February 1962
Phoenix Hall

Weber: Overture, 'Der Freischütz
Ravel: Pavane for a Dead Infanta
Beethoven: Symphony no 2
Enescu: Symphony no 1*

Edgar Cosma, conductor
**First Irish performance*

Back in Dublin the Autumn 'Subscription' on 4 November saw the welcome return of Hans Schmidt-Isserstedt for Wagner's *The Flying Dutchman* Overture, Duff's Irish Suite, Grieg's Piano Concerto with Charles Lynch and Brahms's Third Symphony.

By 1962 Domenico Galassi, Alexander Marr and Heinz Rittweger (whose own Csárdás Players also gave many broadcasts) were long-standing first violin personnel; Hans Hecker and Jack Leydier in the seconds; Coral Bognuda, Vincenzo Caminiti and Egon Jauch, cellos; Jacques Lavaud in the basses. David Lloyd was principal clarinet and Arno Scheibe among the horns. Giulio Sfingi was principal trumpet; Alfred Stille and Ewe Vieth in the trombones and János Keszei-Koch in the percussion section.

Young Irish musicians included Frances Biggs, Anita Dunkerley (sister of flautist Patricia), Yvonne McGuinness, Margaret McLoughlin, Vanessa McMahon and Sheila O'Grady in the violins; Maureen Carolan, Gertrude Gunn, Deirdre Levins and Pádraig O'Connor in the violas and Moya O'Grady, cello. In the woodwind James Daly and Sydney Egan were clarinets; Tom Briggs and Patrick McElwee adding to the horn section.

Television appearances

With Telefís Éireann now up and running, Tibor Paul availed of the opportunity of presenting the RÉSO to a wider audience and one of the Orchestra's earliest television appearances was in Mozart's Sinfonia Concertante K 364 with the young married couple Audrey Park and Archie Collins as soloists. The idea of young artists continued with cellist Aisling Drury Byrne, fresh from her studies in Paris, seen and heard in the Saint-Saëns Concerto.

Next Veronica McSwiney played the Grieg Piano Concerto for television and this was followed by a programme devoted to the Sibelius *'Valse Triste'* and Rossini's *William Tell* Overture which showed the Orchestra's then principal cellist, Vincenzo Caminiti, well to the fore.

These programmes were directed by Kevin Roche who had been promoted to Assistant Director of Music in 1956. In addition to his duties in radio he had undertaken a training course in television production, specialising in the presentation of orchestral and chamber music. Bill Skinner produced Paul and the Orchestra in Beethoven's Fourth Symphony and much later a screening, produced by Kevin Roche in St Patrick's Training College in Drumcondra, would have the brilliant young Korean violinist, Kyung Wha Chung, in the Tchaikovsky Concerto.

AJ Potter was commissioned to write an opera for television transmission. The result was *Patrick*, set to a libretto by Donagh MacDonagh, but the work, although completed during 1962, took another three years to be screened. It was eventually shown on St Patrick's Day 1965 with Edwin Fitzgibbon as Patrick, a British blitz-baby evacuated to Ireland where he grows up. After manifold visions Patrick returns to Britain to reconvert its populace to Christianity. Bernadette Greevy took the part of a Jamaican nurse; Othmar Remy Arthur was a Jamaican labourer and Martin

Geraldine O'Grady

Geraldine O'Grady comes from a talented family of musicians which includes her sisters, violinist Sheila and cellist Moya, who later joined the ranks of the RÉSO, and pianist Eily, who would accompany her husband, Frank Patterson, on their international career. Recently her daughter, Oonagh Keogh, has stepped into the limelight as a solo violinist. Geraldine O'Grady studied at the Paris Conservatoire, where she was awarded a *premier prix* and three special prizes by an international jury chaired by Arthur Grumiaux. Before her appointment as Leader, Geraldine had already appeared as soloist with the orchestra on a number of occasions. Her first solo spot had been as a very young girl with her teacher at the Paris Conservatoire, Jean Fournier, when under Edouard Lindenberg they played the Bach Double Concerto at the Phoenix Hall on 21 July 1950, Bach's bicentenary year. The *Irish Press* reported on her as 'a promising young player', while Joseph O'Neill in the *Irish Independent* mentioned her 'rich tone and freedom of bowing'. Chausson's Poème under Jean Meylan came on 26 July 1957 and the Beethoven Concerto under Carlo Zecchi on 30 May 1958. Miss O'Grady would lead the orchestra until December 1963, during which time the autocratic hand of Tibor Paul would wield the Principal Conductor's baton. She subsequently developed an extremely successful international career as a recitalist and concert soloist, and as a teacher at the Royal Irish Academy of Music.

Bernadette Greevy

Veronica McSwiney

Dempsey a Native Cornerboy. Tibor Paul conducted the RÉSO, RÉ Singers and Choral Society and Colman Pearce, the young Dublin protégé of Paul, was repetiteur.

Edward Roth was satisfied with the results of music on television and in a piece in the *Irish Press* of 23 January 1963 he explained:

> *'Most nations and communities are composed of a collection of minorities, and the broadcaster recognises that the great majority of people seek in their television viewing - and in this order - entertainment, information and culture. To provide acceptable entertainment, and simultaneously to encourage the general improvement of standards, is a difficult and complex task. Telefís Éireann, despite its shortcomings, has made significant contributions in this area. The Symphony broadcasts have, for example, brought classical music into the homes of many thousands of people who previously had no knowledge of, or interest in, symphonic music'.*

Tibor Paul - the middle years

In one of the first events of 1963 the Orchestra joined the Radio Éireann Choral Society with soloists Cáit Lanigan, soprano, Richard Cooper, tenor and Herbert Moulton, baritone, for the first performance of Brian Boydell's cantata *'Mors et Vita'*, based on William Dunbar and anonymous fifteenth century texts. This took place at the recently rented premises of St Francis Xavier Hall under Paul's baton on 11 January.

There was another first at the Gaiety on 27 January, repeated in Limerick the following evening, when Bernadette Greevy was joined by tenor William McAlpine, replacing the indisposed Richard Lewis, for Mahler's symphonic song cycle *Das Lied von der Erde.* Greevy would undertake the work on many further occasions in Ireland and on the international circuit as time went on.

Limerick was also the venue in February for Beethoven's Ninth Symphony with the Orchestra, Our Lady's Choral Society and Elizabeth Vaughan, Bernadette Greevy, David Galliver and Roger Stalman. With Paul in charge this followed performances in Dublin and Cork, and in yet another Paul spectacular, Dublin's St Patrick's Cathedral was the solemn venue for the Irish premiere of Britten's *War Requiem* on 27 March. This moving and stirring occasion in aid of the Concert Hall Fund had soloists Heather Harper, David Galliver and Donald Bell with the Culwick Choral Society.

In his capacity as Director of Music Paul now decided to abandon the Tuesday studio concerts with audience. These were deemed to be for recording purposes only, which of course would take place during the day. However, the larger space of the SFX Hall (double that of the Phoenix Hall) would probably have been less than full for a concert of just one hour's duration and Paul always preferred a packed house. (The Tuesday events would be occasionally revived but never again became a permanent fixture.) Although the transfer was supposedly of a temporary duration while the Phoenix Hall was being renovated, the orchestra never returned to the Dame Court premises and the building, which had

Igor Stravinsky

Igor Stravinsky with (l) Concerts Manager
Leo Donnelly, (r) **Tibor Paul** and **Geraldine O'Grady,**
arriving at the St Francis Xavier Hall

introduced so many to the orchestral repertoire free of charge, was eventually razed to the ground.

Paul's *pièce de résistance* that year was the Festival of Music and the Arts which was renamed Radio Éireann Festival of Music 1963. Four orchestral concerts were planned - three in Dublin and one in Cork, the latter on 20 June celebrating the 150th anniversary of Wagner's birth. The internationally acclaimed soprano, Astrid Varnay, sang Isolde's 'Liebestod' and Brünnhilde's Immolation Scene. The DGOS also participated with productions of *Aida*, celebrating Verdi's 150th anniversary, and *Tosca* at the Gaiety, and there were a number of recital programmes in the Shelbourne Hotel.

Director General, Kevin McCourt, wrote the following introduction in the brochure announcing the festival:

> *'Radio Éireann has been engaged, in many ways, as the chief custodian of professional music making in Ireland during the past twenty years. Through the activities of the staff orchestras, choirs and string quartet it has organised continuous broadcasting of music by the classical and modern masters, while public concerts in Dublin and the provinces have figured increasingly among its activities.*
>
> *Now, for the first time, Radio Éireann has organised a festival of music to take place in June 1963 thus bringing our country into line with the practice of most European nations in holding at least one major summer music festival.*
>
> *The range of eminent personalities featured in the festival is remarkable. Never before in Ireland has a programme of concerts by such distinguished artists been presented in so short a space of time. The music will pay tribute to the anniversaries of Verdi and Wagner with performances of* Aida *in Dublin and a Wagner evening to be given in Cork.*
>
> *I think I can assure all the overseas visitors to the festival that they will be well rewarded for their journeys by the programmes we have to offer. They will be warmly welcomed by a country long famous for its scenery, its hospitality, its wealth of folk-song and tradition - and now rapidly establishing itself in the international field as a notable centre of concert and operatic activity.'*

The first Dublin concert at the Adelphi Cinema in Middle Abbey Street (demolished in 1996 to accommodate an extension to Arnott's department store and a car park) found the eighty-two year old Igor Stravinsky on the RÉSO podium on 9 June. He conducted his Bach *'Von Himmel Hoch'* Variations and Symphony of Psalms with the Radio Éireann Singers and Choral Society. Beforehand, Stravinsky's amanuensis, Robert Craft, took the baton for the ballet *The Fairy's Kiss*. It was another Paul triumph and an unforgettable affair for all present and involved.

The brilliant American pianist, Van Cliburn, was Paul's soloist in Rachmaninov's Third Concerto on 16 June at the impractical Adelphi which was then the only sizable venue available. The third planned Dublin concert was cancelled as the soloist, the world-renowned violinist, Nathan Milstein, was taken ill. Irish audiences were thereby deprived of hearing him

and enjoying the work of the eminent conductor for that evening, Anatole Fistoulari. Despite the artistic success of the festival it was not to be repeated in future years.

Wagner was commemorated again at the Gaiety on 17 November 1963 when the very rarely heard choral piece *'Das Liebesmahl der Apostel'* was resurrected for the occasion. Paul conducted a combination of choirs, and bass David Ward sang Wotan's Farewell from *Die Walküre.* The conductor returned to the Gaiety pit for several performances of *Tristan und Isolde* at the DGOS Winter Season. They contrasted to his *Marriage of Figaro* during the same period.

The Director of Music's busy year still gave space to two young native conductors, Capt Fred O'Callaghan and Proinnsías Ó Duinn, himself a cellist and whose soloist at the SFX Hall was Coral Bognuda in the Saint-Saëns Concerto. Jean Fournet made a welcome return to the Gaiety on 3 November when John Ogdon gave the first Irish performance of Shostakovich's Second Piano Concerto. The Radio Éireann Singers vocalised alluringly in Debussy's *'Sirènes'* and Ravel's Second 'Daphnis and Chloe' Suite.

Hans Werner Henze, rather neglected by Radio Éireann, had a chance with his *Ondine* ballet score also on 29 March; and an interesting piece, Humphrey Searle's 'Riverrun', with its text drawn from Joyce's *Finnegans Wake,* had Marie Keane as the speaking soloist under Paul on 19 July.

Before leaving 1963 one must refer to the DGOS Spring season which offered six operas, *Un ballo in maschera, La Sonnambula, Rigoletto, Macbeth, Tosca* and *Aida.* Conducted by Ottavio Ziino, *Rigoletto* had Piero Cappuccilli in the title role with Margherita Rinaldi as Gilda and Anna di Stasio as Maddalena. Plinio Clabassi alternated with Feruccio Mazzoli as Sparafucile but all five performances (27, 29 and 31 May, 3 and 7 June) had none other than Luciano Pavarotti as the Duke of Mantua. *Tosca* (8, 11, 14 and 18 June) was conducted by Napoleone Annovazzi with Marina Cucchio as the prima donna. The Cavaradossi was Guiseppe di Stefano and the Scarpia Gian Giacomo Guelfi. A seat in the Gaiety Grand Circle was 10/- [50p, or £5 today].

Radio Telefís Éireann Symphony Orchestra

The orchestra altered its name a little in 1964, adding the word Telefís to its title. The members had changed to a degree as well. Geraldine O'Grady decided to pursue her solo career and resigned her leadership from 31 December 1963. Clodagh McSwiney and Elias Maguire were in the violins, Brighid Mooney among the cellos; Wolfgang Eulitz and Jozsef Racz, basses; Richard West was leading clarinet and Thomas Lisenbee leading trumpet. The Irish players Philip Daly, Patrick Dunleavy (later Manager of the RTÉCO and then Concerts Manager) and Patrick Potts were the trombonists. János Keszei was the timpanist while Friedemann Lembens led the percussion section. William Kane was the orchestral librarian and Val Keogh the omnipresent manager.

9 March 1962
Phoenix Hall

Berlioz: Overture, 'Benvenuto Cellini'
Franck: Symphony in D minor
Debussy: Prélude à l'aprés-midi d'un Faune
Debussy: Jeux

Serge Baudo, conductor

18 November 1962
Gaiety Theatre

Ó Riada: Hercules Dux Ferrariae
Mendelssohn: Violin Concerto
Falla: Suite, Three Cornered Hat
Franck: Symphony in D

Hugh Maguire, violin
Enrique Jorda, conductor
This concert was also performed in Limerick on 19 November

Mozart/Bartók series, 1964
conductor: Tibor Paul

28 February
Mozart: Symphony no 38, K504
Bartók: Rhapsodies nos 1 and 2
Bartók: Suite op.3

János Fürst, violin

6 March
Mozart: Symphony no 39, K543
Bartók: Dance Suite
Bartók: Portraits opp 5 and 10

John Ronayne, violin

13 March
Mozart: Symphony no 40, K550
Bartók: Piano Rhapsody
Bartók: Music for strings, percussion and celeste

Deirdre McNulty, piano

20 March
Mozart: Symphony no 41, K551
Bartók: Piano Concerto no 1
Bartók: Concerto for Orchestra

Rhondda Gillespie, piano

10 April 1964
St Francis Xavier Hall

Richard Strauss: Aus Italien
Daniel McNulty: Piano Concertino*
Seoirse Bodley: Symphony no 1

Deirdre McNulty, piano
Tibor Paul, conductor
**First performance*

May-June 1964
Dublin Grand Opera Society
La traviata

Violetta: Margherita Rinaldi
Flora : Mary Sheridan
Germont père: Guiseppe Taddei
Alfredo: Luciano Pavarotti
Conductor: Ferdinando Guarnieri

Pavarotti also sang Rodolfo in La Bohème with Ivana Tosini as Mimi, conducted by Napoleone Annovazzi

14 February 1965
Gaiety Theatre

Falla: Suite, 'El Amor Brujo'
Brahms: Concerto for Violin and Cello
Dvořák: Symphony no 8

John Ronayne, violin
Bernard Vocadlo, cello
Enrique Jorda, conductor

January 1964 saw the return to Dublin of the Hungarian virtuoso Geza Anda for the Brahms Second Piano Concerto under Paul's direction. At the SFX Hall the studio concerts reverted to Fridays following a Wednesday trial in January.

Concert and Assembly Halls found Paul again immersed in Beethoven with Julius Katchen heard in the Piano Concertos at the National Stadium at the end of April and beginning of May. In unusual choral music, the Orchestra accompanied RTÉ's vocal forces in Honegger's *King David* (Hans Waldemar Rosen) and a repeat of Boydell's *'Mors et Vita'*. Under the composer's hand on 17 April, this performance took place in Marian College in Ballsbridge.

In a spectacular event at the Gaiety on 10 May José Iturbi was the Orchestra's soloist/conductor in Concertos by Mozart (D minor) and Grieg followed by Gershwin's Rhapsody in Blue. Mahler's *Das Lied von der Erde* was revived by Bernadette Greevy, but with Edwin Fitzgibbon in the tenor songs, while, in June, Paul was back in the Gaiety pit with the Orchestra for four exciting performances (4, 6, 10 and 12) of Verdi's *Otello* - his last opera appearances in Dublin.

On 18 September the Principal Conductor was engaged with Richard Strauss at the SFX Hall through *'Tod und Verklärung'*, the 'Burleske' (Veronica McSwiney) and *'Ein Heldenleben'*, but later in the month, on 26th, Tibor Paul brought the Orchestra to Killarney's Town Hall where Bernadette Greevy sang French arias (Thomas and Saint-Saëns). The main work in Killarney was Beethoven's Seventh Symphony preceded by Liszt's *'Les Préludes'*. This was part of the Principal Conductor's policy of touring the RÉSO to as many regional centres as possible. Paul's emphasis on style and his sense of his own status might have made him aloof and remote, and might have drawn the Orchestra into a rarefied atmosphere, but the opposite was in fact the case: indeed, it is said that he was determined to bring it to every town in Ireland, and that one of his few unfulfilled ambitions was to perform in the Church of SS Peter and Paul in Athlone, a request steadfastly refused by the church authorities.

This was the year too when the Government announced it was to honour the late President of the United States, John F Kennedy, by building and dedicating a national concert hall in his memory. A site at Beggar's Bush in Haddington Road was earmarked and purchased and plans prepared. The idea was heartily welcomed by music organisations and music lovers in general and supported by Radio Éireann's Director of Music. However it left Concert and Assembly Halls in a small quandary as it had a growing fund which it would now be obliged to disperse. It also ended the promotion of concerts and recitals with the specific objective of raising money for a new hall. That the Hall did not materialise until 1981 and on a different site is another matter entirely. A profile of Tibor Paul in the *RTV Guide* (29 October 1965) told us:

> *'Immediately his care is for the future of music in Ireland. He is attempting to build an audience for the Kennedy Hall so that in three years time people will be ready for it, educated for the many, many concerts which must take*

25 June 1965
St Francis Xavier Hall

Haydn:	Symphony no 94 ('Surprise')
Joonan Kokkonen:	Sinfonia da camera*
Stamitz:	Viola Concerto
Wagner:	Prelude, Act 1, *Lohengrin*
Wagner:	Prelude & Liebestod, *Tristan und Isolde*
Wagner:	Overture, *Tannhäuser*

Anthony Byrne, viola
Tibor Paul, conductor
**First Irish performance*

17 October 1965
Gaiety Theatre

Weber:	Overture, 'Oberon'
Victory:	Pariah-Music*
Rachmaninov:	Rhapsody on a theme of Paganini
Stravinsky:	The Rite of Spring

Shura Cherkassky, piano
Tibor Paul, conductor
**First performance*

9 July 1965
St Francis Xavier Hall

Haydn:	Symphony no 100 ('Military')
Honegger:	Concerto da camera
Franck:	Symphony in D minor

André Prieur, flute,
Helmut Seeber, oboe
Tibor Paul, conductor

14 January 1966
St Francis Xavier Hall

Richard Strauss:	Tod und Verklärung
Brian Boydell:	Violin Concerto
Beethoven:	Symphony no 4

Geraldine O'Grady, violin
Tibor Paul, conductor

> *place there if it is to be a practical proposition.'*

Naturally there were problems. Paul was quoted as saying

> *'The Kennedy Hall is a big project, costing £2.5 million. We must start in the schools. I am giving more and more school concerts - last week, 1,700 children at one concert in Wexford. Three or four years ago, the Gaiety concert audiences were mostly adults. Now the half is youth. The 200 seats in the Phoenix Hall were seldom full, today at the Francis Xavier Hall 800 seats are filled every Friday. The hall is in a very bad area but still they are there - young people with scores in their hands.'*

Tibor Paul - the final years

After the hectic activity of the previous two years, 1965 seems to have been less adventurous, although Prokofiev's Fifth Piano Concerto (Sergiu Petricaroli) and the Britten Piano Concerto (Margaret Kitchen) were heard in the SFX Hall. Paul conducted on 8 and 15 January and Carl Orff's *Carmina Burana*, not then as popular as it is today, tended to retain the air of enterprise as did the premiere of Seán Ó Riada's 'Nomos 2' at the SFX Hall on 23 April. The composer had been working on the piece for almost seven years, finishing it in 1963. His text was taken from a number of the Theban plays of Sophocles, translated by EF Watling. The large-scale work had Herbert Moulton, the RTÉ Singers and Choral Society actively involved. On a smaller scale Paul and the Orchestra gave a concert of music by Haydn ('Schoolmaster' Symphony) and Bach (E major Harpsichord Concerto with John Beckett) in the United States Embassy in Ballsbridge in September.

The eminent German pianist, Wilhelm Kempff, was Paul's soloist on 3 October in Beethoven's 'Emperor' and, in an unprecedented step on the evening following this Gaiety Subscription concert, Kempff played the Schumann Concerto at the SFX Hall. For this event only there was an admission charge to a studio concert. Both events proved to be magnificent affairs.

Outside Dublin, on 23 October 1965, the Wexford Festival introduced the Vienna-born, Prague-based conductor Albert Rosen to Ireland. It was a remarkable début in Massenet's *Don Quichotte* with the aging but magnificent Miroslav Cangalovic in the title role. Albert Rosen would retain his association with the Orchestra for the next thirty-two years, ending only with his death in May 1997. Among his many opera triumphs would be *The Bartered Bride* at the DGOS in 1971, and, at Wexford, *Káta Kabanová* and *The Turn of the Screw.*

The fiftieth anniversary of Easter Week 1916 was celebrated by a number of significant events nationwide. The orchestra played its part on Easter Monday 1966 with Brian Boydell's commissioned 'A Terrible Beauty is Born'. Its text, compiled by Tomás Ó Súilleabháin, was taken from a number of native sources including WB Yeats, Thomas MacDonagh and Tom Kettle. Paul conducted and invited Our Lady's Choral Society, celebrating its own coming of age, to take part.

25 March 1966
St Francis Xavier Hall

Bartók: Divertimento
Victory: Five Mantras
Wolf: Harper Songs
Brahms: Symphony no 2

Austin Gaffney, baritone
Tibor Paul, conductor

1 July 1966
St Francis Xavier Hall

Sibelius: Symphony no 1
Richard Rodney Bennett: Symphony*
Halffter: Canticum in PP Johannem XXIII*

Patricia McCarry, soprano
Austin Gaffney, baritone
St James's Gate Musical Society Choir
Tibor Paul, conductor
**First Irish performance*

29 January 1967
Gaiety Theatre

Seoirse Bodley: Configurations*
Rachmaninov: Piano Concerto no 3
Stravinsky: Symphony of Psalms

Alicia de Larrocha, piano
Guinness Choir
Tibor Paul, conductor
**First performance*

5 April 1967
St Patrick's Cathedral

Britten: War Requiem

Veronica Dunne, soprano
Kenneth Bowen, tenor
Peter McBrien, bass-baritone
RTÉ Singers and Choral Society
Associate conductor, Seoirse Bodley
Tibor Paul, conductor

13 April 1967
Dublin Castle

Handel: Messiah

Agnes Giebel, soprano
Bernadette Greevy, contralto
Frank Patterson, tenor
John Shirley-Quirk, bass
Our Lady's Choral Society
Tibor Paul, conductor
to celebrate the 225th anniversary of the work's first performance (Dublin, 1742)

5 May 1967
St Francis Xavier Hall

Henk Badings: Concerto for two pianos
Richard Strauss: Ein Heldenleben

Franz-Josef Hirt and Gisela Ungerer, pianos
Tibor Paul, conductor

The soloists were Veronica Dunne, Bernadette Greevy and William Young, another singer who would continue to have a significant role in the world of oratorio for many years. The performance was also televised and 'A Terrible Beauty is Born' was repeated in the SFX Hall with the same artists on 8 July and, as at the premiere, was preceded by Beethoven's 'Eroica' Symphony.

As part of its own 21st anniversary season, Our Lady's Choral Society had taken part in Beethoven's Ninth Symphony at the Gaiety the previous week. The soloists were Irene Sandford, Bernadette Greevy, Edwin Fitzgibbon and Harold Gray. The Society's actual 21st Birthday concert was at the RDS on 3 September, when Tibor Paul conducted the choir and RÉSO in the Berlioz *Requiem*. Edwin Fitzgibbon was the tenor soloist and the specially commissioned setting of the 'Hail Mary' from AJ Potter featured Bernadette Greevy with the choir.

In the earlier Subscription concerts Paul introduced Bartók's *Duke Bluebeard's Castle* to Dublin on 5 February with Marilyn Tyler as the doomed Judith and Derrik Olsen as the hapless Bluebeard. Two weeks later the eminent Henryk Szeryng was Paul's soloist in the Brahms Violin Concerto but the planned Bruckner Seventh Symphony that evening had to be replaced by Beethoven's Seventh as an influenza epidemic depleted the orchestral ranks.

The DGOS celebrated its 25th anniversary with an Italian Season at the Gaiety between May and June. The Orchestra accompanied the five operas, *Don Pasquale, Tosca, La traviata, Il trovatore* and *Rigoletto,* with conductors Napoleone Annovazzi and Guiseppe Morelli assisted by Valentino Barcellesi. The casts included Luisa Maragliano, Margherita Rinaldi, Ugo Benelli, Renato Bruson, Attilio d'Orazi, Piero Cappuccilli and Paolo Washington.

A special concert at the Gaiety on 10 July was outside the normal Subscription season and focused on the great cellist, Mstislav Rostropovich, whom Paul had managed to engage for the Dvořák Concerto. With Tchaikovsky's 'Pathétique' Symphony, it was another of those splendid occasions in which the conductor, and indeed everyone else present, revelled. This concert was initially planned for the RDS on 24 June but was postponed due to the illness of Rostropovich. Ticket prices ranged from 5/- to 30/- [25p to £1.50].

Tibor Paul scheduled the orchestra for a special Members' Concert at the Royal Dublin Society on 7 October 1966. Just before it, he received a communication from RTÉ Director General, Kevin McCourt, a man not known for his tolerance of the Director of Music in the corridors of power in RTÉ. Unfortunately, Paul's attitude, as well as the extravagant expenditure of his department's activities, had not ingratiated him with many of his peers within the management structure.

In effect McCourt's letter informed Tibor Paul that his contract would not be renewed when it expired the following year. He would be offered three months' guest appearances with the Orchestra for a period of time. With true professionalism, Paul conducted the RDS concert in which Deirdre McNulty gave the first Irish performance of the Tippett

1966 – British press reaction

Edward Greenfield of *The Guardian* wrote:

"This is a highly civilised, stylish body, well capable of taking virtuoso scores by Bartók and Mahler in its stride....Tibor Paul showed his players' refinement from the very start of the Bartók Concerto for Orchestra with a string tremolo hushed to the merest whisper...there was never any doubt of the complete authenticity of Paul's reading. In both the Bartók and Mahler one sensed that the Orchestra was very much on its best behaviour, but after the interval Brahms's Symphony No 1 brought a warmer style, but marked by specially beautiful string tone".

From *The Times:*

"The programme was nicely calculated to show the tonal and virtuoso qualities of the orchestra...The string sound muscular rather than silken, though there were places in Bartók's Concerto for Orchestra and in Brahms's 1st Symphony where warm tone is called for, and was forthcoming. The woodwind choir....contains some sensitive soloists, notably the first oboe, who gave a captivating account of Brahms's solo passages".

In *The Financial Times* David Cairns wrote:

"Mr Paul has built up a strong predominantly young band, with a good sonority to it ; the strings (with double-basses bowing in the continental style) make a substantial sound, the cellos play with a singing line, and the violins are capable of fresh, warm, sappy tone and incisive attack.

From *The Daily Express* critic, Alan Blyth, came:

"The warmth of the strings, precision of the woodwind, and mellowness of the brass were on display in Bartók's eventful Concerto for Orchestra. Then in Brahms's First Symphony they merged as a deeply satisfying entity. Here the rich results of always playing as an ensemble under a skilled, intelligent conductor were clear".

Writing in *The Sunday Times* Desmond Shawe-Taylor commented:

"It is an orchestra of predominantly soft contours; light, bright winds, warm strings with plenty of body, full but not overpowering brass; the whole well blended and balanced. They brought a delightfully supple rhythm to the fourth movement of Bartók's Concerto for Orchestra, and excelled in the two middle movements of the First Brahms Symphony. In Mahler's "Kindertotenlieder" Bernadette Greevy displayed a warm and smooth contralto and a musicianly sense of phrase".

Piano Concerto, but with almost dramatic effect he suffered a heart attack soon after and had to be hospitalised. There was an amount of press coverage, and flowers sent by McCourt to the Mater Private Nursing Home were returned. However, the conductor recovered sufficiently to lead the Orchestra to one of its, hitherto, finest achievements - its first journey across the Irish Sea.

Concerts in the UK

A concert at London's Royal Festival Hall on 30 November was part of the Royal Philharmonic Society's 1966/67 season and it exposed the RTÉSO to the international limelight. It was an historic occasion which gave the Orchestra an added boost to its morale. Autocratic, charismatic, egotistical, energetic and even tyrannical as Paul may have been, and while he may have promoted himself as much as the RTÉSO (Charles Acton, then music critic of *The Irish Times,* once described Paul as 'the pastmaster of the great occasion'), this Royal Festival Hall concert and another one the following day for BBC TV at the Fairfield Hall in Croydon established the Orchestra abroad as Ireland's major musical force.

The RFH programme, previewed at the SFX Hall before departure, was Bartók's Concerto for Orchestra, Mahler's *Kindertotenlieder* with Bernadette Greevy, and Brahms's First Symphony.

The Croydon concert was transmitted by BBC TV on 8 December. Bernadette Greevy and Geraldine O'Grady were the soloists with Miss Greevy giving a group of Irish songs including 'Wee Hughie' by JF Larchet, who was present, and Harty's 'Sea Wrack'. Geraldine O'Grady played the Chausson *'Poème'.* The programme opened with the brilliant Strauss tone poem *'Don Juan'* and closed with the colourful 'Sorcerer's Apprentice' by Dukas. Tibor Paul and the Orchestra, understandably highly elated, returned to Dublin immediately after the television concert. Much of the arranging of this tour was handled with great efficiency by the Concerts Manager since 1956, Leo Donnelly, working tirelessly in what was uncharted territory.

However, despite all his and the RTÉSO's triumphs, 1966 must have been Tibor Paul's *annus horribilis.* The next year saw his departure from Dublin but not before several interesting programmes.

Tibor Paul retired from RTÉ and the Irish music scene in a blaze of glory through another Beethoven cycle at the SFX Hall during July 1967. His soloists in the First, Third, Fourth and Fifth Piano Concertos were Veronica McSwiney, Anthony Hughes, Charles Lynch and Darina Gibson. The venue could not accommodate all those wishing to attend the final concert of the Eighth and Ninth Symphonies on 28th and several hundred were unable to obtain admission. Our Lady's Choral Society was again the favoured choir with Irene Sandford, Bernadette Greevy, Edwin Fitzgibbon and Harold Gray.

Audience reception in the circumstances was ecstatic and Maud Aiken, one of 2RN's early Station Orchestra violinists, an enthusiastic supporter of the conductor and wife of the then Minister for Foreign Affairs, gave a highly laudatory oration. Tibor Paul graciously responded. He did not conduct in Ireland again, spending

Gerard Victory

Philip Martin

much of the next six years in Australia where he died in November 1973.

Gerard Victory becomes Director of Music

The first public concert following Paul's departure was conducted, significantly, by Eimear Ó Broin, who had found himself somewhat marginalised during the previous Director of Music's tenure of office. The concert on 1 September 1967 had a youthful twist to it with the twenty-year old Philip Martin playing Gershwin's Piano Concerto. The programme two weeks later was to be suddenly truncated when the scheduled soloist, Pietro Spada, was taken ill. This meant Martinů's Fifth Symphony stood alone under Colman Pearce's baton.

Visiting conductors to the Autumn Subscription concerts included Enrique Jorda, Édouard van Remoortel and Alceo Galliera, with matching soloists Martha Argerich (Ravel's Piano Concerto), Tamas Vasary (Chopin's Second) and the veteran Alfredo Campoli (Mendelssohn's Violin Concerto). The Winter DGOS Season again relied on its Bucharest connection for *Mignon, Carmen* and *Werther.* Napoleone Annovazzi conducted.

Further changes in orchestral personnel found Timothy Kirwan and Thérèse Timoney in the violins; Margaret Healy and Séamus O'Grady, violas; Albin Berky, Christine Cooley and Claude Fort, cellos, and Helmut Engemann was leading the double-basses. Patricia Dunkerley had joined the flautists, Lindsay Armstrong the oboes, and Carole Block the bassoons. Her husband Colin was in the horn section; Jozsef Csibi led the trumpets, where Szabolcs Vedres, who would marry violinist Clodagh McSwiney, also sat. In time their daughter, Anita, would be in the Orchestra with her mother. Constantin Avgerinos was timpanist in place of János Keszei. A number of musicians had left the Orchestra during 1966 to join the newly established Ulster Orchestra in Belfast but some would return.

The RTÉSO now lacked a Director of Music and a principal conductor but the interregnum was relatively short. Gerard Victory, who had been Deputy Director of Music under Tibor Paul, took over as Director in 1967 with Kevin Roche appointed as Deputy Director at the same time. Victory was an extraordinary man. A graduate of UCD in Celtic Studies and Modern Languages, he spoke several fluently. He was working in the Central Statistics Office and making music a part-time occupation before he joined the Radio Éireann Players.

He remained as Director of Music until 1984, when he retired to devote himself to composition. During his tenure the RTÉSO enjoyed a period of incredible diversity. Victory was accused by some of usurping his position to have his own music performed but this is far from the truth. While Victory had a remarkable facility to compose and his output was legion, nevertheless, a check of the Orchestra's programmes during his period as Director will show a remarkable cross-section of the work of other Irish composers.

Albert Rosen

Albert Rosen was born on 14 February 1924 in Vienna and educated in Prague, where he became Resident Conductor of the Prague National Opera in 1965, and Director of the Smetana Opera. In addition to his work as Principal Conductor of the RTÉSO and later as Chief Guest Conductor and Conductor Laureate, he worked extensively in opera, conducting 165 opera performances (140 in Dublin and 25 in Cork) of twenty-four operas for the DGOS and a further eighteen works for the Wexford Festival, the last of which was Leoncavallo's *La Bohème* in 1994. In December 1973 he gave the first Irish performances of Janácek's *Jenůfa* at the Gaiety.

He subsequently became Principal Conductor of the five orchestras of the Australian Broadcasting Corporation, and his career in opera brought him further acclaim in San Francisco, San Diego *(Russalka)* and with English National Opera for Rimsky-Korsakov's *Christmas Eve*. He is also remembered for his developmental work with the National Youth Orchestra of Ireland.

Albert Rosen as principal conductor

On the conducting front, Albert Rosen had been creating a considerable impression at the Wexford Festival where he had just completed a series of performances of the 'rival' *Otello* (Rossini). He was duly considered for the position of Principal Conductor and eventually invited to accept the post on a contractual basis from January 1969. This he did and, as has been mentioned, his association with the Orchestra continued until 1997. He remained as Principal until the end of 1980, the longest holder of the position to date, when he became Chief Guest Conductor. From his seventieth birthday in 1994 until his death in 1997 Albert Rosen was the Orchestra's Conductor Laureate. On that occasion he was presented with a citation which read in part:

> *'Albert Rosen has earned a privileged place within the music profession in Ireland and in the affection of Irish music lovers....He has brought his immense international reputation to the service of music-making in Ireland which he has developed and enhanced and has thereby achieved the acclaim of audiences at home and throughout Europe'.*

Albert Rosen found the atmosphere in Dublin much more congenial than the rigours of the state system in Prague, where he was director of the Smetana Opera House and conductor at the National Theatre. Almost at once he set about broadening his orchestral repertoire. He would continue the policy of Milan Horvat and Tibor Paul in programming works by Irish composers. Indeed among his earliest 'pre-appointment' concerts, Seoirse Bodley's 'Music for Strings' can be found on the menu for 19 January 1968, and he would retain the policy of offering orchestral members solo engagements. This may have been spurred on by principal trumpet, Joszef Csibi, being heard in the Hummel Concerto on 27 January at the SFX Hall.

The challenge of Honegger's *St Joan of Arc* at the Stake was accepted and successfully upheld at the Gaiety on 11 February. This work for singers and actors, with the remarkable Eithne Dunne as Joan, showed Albert Rosen's innate sense of dramatic energy, something which would remain a hallmark of his performances throughout his long career in Radio Éireann and elsewhere.

There was still room for many other visiting conductors during 1968, among them Gunnar Staern, Piero Bellugi and Erich Riede who directed a Palm Sunday account of Bach's *St Matthew Passion.* This Gaiety performance with the Guinness Choir on 7 April had Frank Patterson as the impeccable Evangelist and Claus Ocker the dignified Christus.

With Sydney Bryans on the rostrum, Our Lady's Choral Society added Walton's *Belshazzar's Feast* to its repertoire on 15 March, while the Limerick Choral Union engaged the Orchestra for Janáček's *Glagolitic Mass* at the city's Savoy Cinema on 26 April. The conductor from Bratislava was L'udovit Rajter, then in charge of the Slovak Philharmonic, with soloists Veronica Dunne, Mary Sheridan, William McAlpine and Patrick McGuigan.

31 March 1967
St Francis Xavier Hall

Beethoven: Fidelio
[concert performance by Irish National Opera]

Leonora:	Dolores Burke
Florestan:	Edwin Fitzgibbon
Marcellina:	Mary Sheridan
Jaquino:	Patrick Ring
Pizarro:	William Young
Rocco:	Martin Dempsey
Don Fernando:	Gerald Duffy

St Peter's Male Voice Choir, Drogheda
RTÉ Choral Society
Tibor Paul, conductor

10 March 1968
Gaiety Theatre

Walton:	Overture, 'Portsmouth Point'
Gerard Schurmann:	'Chuench'i'
Prokofiev:	Piano Concerto no 3
Beethoven:	Symphony no 7

Ank Reinders, soprano
John Browning, piano
Gerard Schurmann, conductor
This concert was repeated in Cork on 11 March

24 March 1968
Gaiety Theatre

Ó Riada:	Hercules Dux Ferrariae
Bruch:	Violin Concerto no 1
Mahler:	Symphony no 1

Mary Gallagher, violin
Piero Bellugi, conductor

3 May 1968
St Francis Xavier Hall

Haydn:	Symphony no 103 ('Drum Roll')
Bach:	Concerto for two violins
Honegger:	Pacific 231
Liebermann:	Concerto for Jazz band and orchestra*

Geraldine and Sheila O'Grady, violins
Colman Pearce, conductor
**First Irish performance*

Napoleone Annovazzi

Contemporary music

1969 brought the Dublin 20th Century Festival into being. Under the auspices of the Music Association of Ireland, it found Radio Éireann actively involved. The orchestral concert at the SFX Hall on 7 January was conducted by Gerard Schurmann and had Charles Lynch, John McCabe, the English pianist/composer, and James Blades, timpani, as soloists. They were heard in Martinů's Concerto for Double String Orchestra, Piano and Timpani, and Alan Rawsthorne's Two Piano Concerto. Schurmann included his own 'Seven Studies of Francis Bacon' and allowed Seoirse Bodley to direct his own Symphony for Chamber Orchestra.

The following year, 1970, saw the RTÉSO in two concerts in the Dublin Festival of 20th Century Music. The first, on 4 January, was conducted by Seoirse Bodley and Hans Waldemar Rosen and included John Kinsella's 'Rondo', Bodley's 'Divertimento', Ó Riada's 'Greek Epigrams' and the first Irish performance of Peter Maxwell Davies's *'Veni Sancti Spiritus'* with the RTÉ Singers. The second programme on 9 January saw the return of Gerard Schurmann to conduct. Prokofiev's First Violin Concerto was played by Yossi Zivoni and followed by Stravinsky's Symphony in Three Movements. As we shall see shortly, a considerable range of twentieth century works, from the well-established to the avant-garde, continued to feature in the Orchestra's schedules, both as part of the Dublin festival and in its regular concert programmes.

Albert Rosen was now actively engaged with the RTÉSO. At the Spring Subscriptions he directed a number of highly fascinating programmes. These included a 'meticulously prepared' premiere of Brian Boydell's 'Symphonic Inscapes' on 26 January; Stravinsky's *Oedipus Rex* had RTÉ's own choral forces and a cast that included Alexander Young in the title role, Bernadette Greevy as Jocasta and Kim Borg as Tiresias on 9 February; the Berlioz oratorio *L'Enfance du Christ* came the next week with Our Lady's Choral Society, Mary Sheridan, Frank Patterson, Eric Hinds and Youri Kesselhorf. The performance was repeated in Cork from where it was televised and shown at a later date. The premiere of AJ Potter's 'Sinfonia De Profundis' was coupled with the first Irish performance of Ginastera's Harp Concerto with the renowned Nicanor Zabaleta on 23 March. Later in the year AJ Potter was honoured with a Jacob's Award for his 'most striking contribution to serious music'.

Moving to the Autumn Subscription series, Robert Casadesus was Rosen's eminent soloist in Beethoven's 'Emperor' Concerto on 6 October, while the young Jean Rodolphe Kars, who would later abandon his career for the Catholic priesthood, gave an ethereal account of the Tchaikovsky First Concerto on 23 November 1969. In between, Rosen took the Orchestra to Limerick with Ivan Davis for Brahms's First Piano Concerto and Stravinsky's *Petrushka* on the 10th and with the RTÉ Choral Society and Patrick Ring, tenor, brought Liszt's 'Faust' Symphony to the Gaiety on the 16th.

In some other unusual scheduling that year, Patricia Dunkerley and Helmut Seeber played a Flute and Oboe Concerto by Cimarosa on 28 March and, under Ole Schmidt, the Danish accordionist Mogens Ellegaard gave the first performance of Gerard Victory's

24 May 1968
St Francis Xavier Hall

Liebermann: Furioso
Roussel: Bacchus and Ariadne
Bruckner: Symphony no 4

Napoleone Annovazzi, conductor

19 July 1968
St Francis Xavier Hall

Mozart: Symphony no 41, K551
Bloch: Violin Concerto
Debussy: Nocturnes, 'Nuages', 'Fetes'
Dukas: The Sorcerer's Apprentice

Brendan O'Brien, violin
Pierre Colombo, conductor

6 September 1968
St Francis Xavier Hall

Haydn: Symphony no 92 ('Oxford')
Barber: Piano Concerto*
Sibelius: Return of Lemminkainen
Blomdahl: Symphony no 2*

Philip Martin, piano
Eimear Ó Broin, conductor
**First Irish performance*

13 September 1968
St Francis Xavier Hall

Beethoven: Overture, Leonora no 2
Mozart: Adagio & Fugue, K546
Bartók: Piano Concerto no 3
Bartók: Concerto for Orchestra

Charles Lynch, piano
György Lehel, conductor

20 September 1968
St Francis Xavier Hall

Mozart: Symphony no 36, K425
Richard Strauss: Violin Concerto
Stravinsky: Symphony in Three Movements

John Ronayne, violin
Colman Pearce, conductor

27 September 1968
St Francis Xavier Hall

Schoenberg: Five Orchestral Pieces* (1949)
Beethoven: Piano Concerto no 4
Stravinsky: Petrushka

Lotte Jekeli, piano
Edgar Cosma, conductor
**First Irish performance*

6 October 1968
Gaiety Theatre

Bach/Stokowski: Toccata & Fugue in D minor
Rachmaninov: Rhapsody on a theme of Paganini
Ravel: La Valse
Schubert: Symphony no 9

Augustin Anievas, piano
Constantin Silvestri, conductor
This concert was repeated in Cork on 7 October

13 October 1968
Gaiety Theatre

Wangenheim: Sonatina*
Beethoven: Piano Concerto no 1
Beethoven: Symphony no 7

Florence Wild, piano
Volker Wangenheim, conductor
**First Irish performance*

10 November 1968
Gaiety Theatre

Brahms: Tragic Overture
Tchaikovsky: Violin Concerto
Tchaikovsky: Fantsay-overture, Romeo and Juliet
Kodály: Háry János suite

Josef Sivo, violin
Peter Erös, conductor

Concerto. The work was commissioned by Ellegaard and dedicated to him. Other commissions followed, including a concerto for two accordions by James Wilson, a rare example of an instrument then not widely regarded as a classical concert solo - matched perhaps only by Larry Adler performing the Romanian Fantasy for Harmonica and Orchestra by Francis Chagrin (1975).

Yvonne McGuinness and Brian Mack, of the first violins and violas respectively, were heard in Mozart's Sinfonia Concertante with Eimear Ó Broin on 30 May; and Vincenzo Caminiti, then the Orchestra's principal cello, premiered John Kinsella's Concerto with Sydney Bryans on 6 June. Other modern and contemporary works from this period include Jiri Pauer's then recent Horn Concerto on 12 September (Victor Malíř, with Erich Böhlke directing), and on 16 September Hindemith's 'Sinfonia Serena' conducted by André Prieur.

Albert Rosen directed the premiere of Raymond Warren's First Symphony on 19 June, Martinů's Sixth Symphony on 10 July, and introduced the Second Symphony of Henri Dutilleux to Dublin on 17 July. Another performance of AJ Potter's 'Sinfonia De Profundis' came on 8 November, with Bartók's Music for Strings, Percussion and Celesta, also at the Gaiety, the following week.

The 1971 Dublin Festival of 20th Century Music included two orchestral concerts on 8 and 12 January at the SFX Hall. The first programme included the premiere of the song cycle 'Never to have loved is best' by Seoirse Bodley. This RTÉ commission for the WB Yeats centenary was sung by Veronica Dunne. The other soloist was the acclaimed Lothar Faber who was heard in a work written specially for him in 1967 - Bruno Maderna's Second Oboe Concerto. The conductor was Pierre Michel le Conte and the main work was Stravinsky's *The Rite of Spring.*

Proinnsías Ó Duinn directed the other concert, making Shostakovich's Tenth Symphony its focal point. It followed Krzysztof Penderecki's 'Threnody' and John Kinsella's 'Montage II'. Mogens Ellegaard was the soloist in Ole Schmidt's Symphonic Fantasy and Allegro for accordion. Less than a week later Ó Duinn continued the contemporary trend with his own First Symphony and Shostakovich's First Cello Concerto with Erling Bløndal Bengtsson at the Gaiety on the 17th. After many years the Orchestra welcomed Jean Martinon back for a Gaiety Subscription on 31 January. The programme included his own Irish Symphony as well as Schumann's Fourth and the concert marked Martinon's last appearance in Dublin.

Another French musician, Charles Brück, took the rostrum on 28 February to give the first performance in Ireland of Penderecki's 'De Natura Sonoris' before David Lillis played the Beethoven Violin Concerto. The RTÉ Choral Society then launched into Kodály's *Psalmus Hungaricus.*

Albert Rosen continued the trend of modernity with the distinguished Ruggiero Ricci in the Ginastera Violin Concerto at the Gaiety on 14 March. Scriabin's *'Poème d'Extase'* was one of those richly romantic scores in which Mr Rosen excelled.

Our Lady's Choral Society: 25th Anniversary Season, 1970

National Stadium

13 May	16 May
Elgar: The Dream of Gerontius	Verdi: Requiem
Janice Chapman, soprano	
Bernadette Greevy, contralto	Bernadette Greevy, contralto
Ronald Dowd, tenor	Ronald Dowd, tenor
David Ward, bass	David Ward, bass
Sir John Barbirolli, conductor	Sir John Barbirolli, conductor

20 November	18 December
St Francis Xavier Hall	National Stadium
Beethoven: Symphony no 9	Handel: Messiah
Mary Sheridan, soprano	Ann Murray, soprano
Bernadette Greevy, contralto	Mary Sheridan, contralto
Louis Browne, tenor	Patrick Ring, tenor
William Young, bass	Thomas Lawler, bass
Albert Rosen, conductor	Albert Rosen, conductor

---

23 January 1970
St Francis Xavier Hall

Brian Boydell: Violin Concerto
Dvořák: Symphony no 7

John Kitchen, violin
Colman Pearce, conductor

22 March 1970
Gaiety Theatre

Dvořák: Requiem

Marjorie Wright, soprano
Bernadette Greevy, contralto
Louis Browne, tenor
Jaroslav Horáček, bass
Guinness Choir
RTÉ Singers
RTÉ Choral Society
Albert Rosen, conductor

22 May 1970
St Francis Xavier Hall

Victory: Praeludium for wind, organ and percussion*
Nielsen: Clarinet Concerto
Beethoven: Symphony no 2

Keith Puddy, clarinet
Michael Casey, organ
Veronica McSwiney, piano
Albert Rosen, conductor
**First performance*

4 October 1970
Gaiety Theatre

Copland: Outdoor Overture
Rachmaninov: Piano Concerto no 2
Tchaikovsky: Symphony no 4

Jeffrey Siegel, piano
Arthur Fiedler, conductor

20 January 1974
Gaiety Theatre

Isang Yun: Réak
Liszt: Piano Concerto no 2
Schubert: Symphony no 9

Witold Malcuzinski, piano
Alfred Walter, conductor
This concert was repeated in Cork on 21 January

17 February 1974
Gaiety Theatre

Richard Strauss: Don Juan
Ravel: Piano Concerto for the left hand
Shostakovich: Symphony no 10

Vlado Perlemuter, piano
Colman Pearce, conductor

Aloys Fleischmann conducted the orchestral version of his own 'Cornucopia' with Victor Malíř on 11 June and another orchestral horn player, Colin Block, took over the rostrum on 14 September for the Brahms Second Symphony and 'Chimaerae' by Derek Ball. Earlier, on 30 July, Proinnsías Ó Duinn decided, for a change, to air the Leopold Stokowski version of Mussorgsky's 'Pictures at an Exhibition' while Colman Pearce brought Ligeti's *'Atmosphères'* to the Gaiety on 10 October.

The MAI's Dublin Festival of 20th Century Music moved to June in 1972 and took the Orchestra suitably into St Patrick's Cathedral for the premiere of Gerard Victory's symphonic portrait 'Jonathan Swift' which Albert Rosen conducted on 24th. The concert revived Brian Boydell's *'Mors et Vita'* with Irene Sandford, Frank Patterson, William Young and the RTÉ Singers and Choral Society. The second concert on the 30th had Colman Pearce directing Bernadette Greevy in the first performance of Seoirse Bodley's 'Meditations on Lines from Patrick Kavanagh' and Charles Lynch in Bartók's Second Piano Concerto.

In the week before the Festival Albert Rosen had conducted Sheila and Moya O'Grady in AJ Potter's Fantasia Concertante and in the week after it gave a glowing account of Schoenberg's *Pelleas und Melisande* at the SFX Hall. Patrick McElwee from the Orchestra's horn section was Mr Rosen's soloist in the Hindemith Concerto on 22 September.

Early in 1973 the orchestra gave the first Irish performance of Shostakovich's Fifteenth Symphony and on 14 January at the Gaiety John Ogdon was Proinnsías Ó Duinn's soloist in the first performance of Gerard Schurmann's Movement for Piano and Orchestra. Ogdon, who was undergoing severe mental stress at the time, also played Liszt's Totentanz and in tragic circumstances attempted suicide the following day.

The year 1971 also saw the departure of John Kitchen from the leader's chair, leaving it to be shared by Arthur Nachstern, John Ronayne and Joseph Maher until the appointment of Dubliner Colin Staveley in January 1974.

Vladimir Ashkenazy came to the Gaiety Subscription concert on 1 October 1972 with Beethoven's Fourth Piano Concerto which Rosen coupled with Mahler's Fifth Symphony. (The concert was repeated in Cork the following evening.) Two weeks later Janáček's Sinfonietta roused the Gaiety rafters. It followed the premiere of James Wilson's *'Le Bateau Ivre'* and Lalo's Symphonie espagnole with Geraldine O'Grady.

Changing personnel

The Orchestral personnel had naturally gone through a considerable transformation in its first twenty-five years but Alice Brough, Dora Hall, Alfonso Evangelisti, Arthur Nachstern and William Shanahan had stood the test of time. Síle Larchet (harp) was now Síle Cuthbert and had left and returned in the intervening period.

New faces included Catherine Briscoe, Teresa Costello, Sunniva Fitzpatrick, Anna Kane and Una Kindlon in the violins. Archie Collins was leading the violas in February 1973 (Máire Larchet

John Kitchen

being on leave of absence) and the section also included John Adams and Margaret Healy.

Paula O'Callaghan, Hilary O'Donovan, Linda Krause and Robert Pierce had joined the cellos and Eamonn Williams and Philomena Madden were in the double-bass line-up. The woodwind had Michael Rogers, bassoon, and the brass included David Carmody, horn, and Eric Dunlea, trumpet. Seán Cahill was leading trombone, with David Weakley next to him; Henning Knöbel was timpanist, with Joachim Weiland leading the percussion section.

The first quarter-century had seen considerable growth and change. Many of the continental musicians who arrived in Dublin in the late 1940s and throughout the 1950s had made their homes in Ireland and become Irish citizens. Their excellent teaching skills had encouraged countless young people to either make their careers in music or to simply enjoy the art of music as a way of relaxation.

The Orchestra had benefitted in different ways from its three Principal Conductors - Horvat, Paul and Rosen - who placed their own particular stamp on the style of playing and performances. The extraordinary range of the Orchestra's repertoire was phenomenal and, if this history highlights the vast contemporary offerings, it should be remembered that a staple diet of the classical, from Haydn to Schubert, and the romantic composers had given the musicians a firm grounding in the techniques of symphonic tradition.

Tibor Paul's initiative in bringing the Orchestra to London in 1966 broke its chain of confinement to the island of Ireland and expanded its horizons. The advancement of television brought the RTÉSO into countless country-wide households where symphonic orchestral music was unfamiliar. But television had a detrimental effect on the Orchestra's touring possibilities in Ireland. Cinemas began to close, thereby depriving the RTÉSO of many of its regional venues. Only the main centres of Limerick and Cork were now being visited with any regularity. However, the first quarter-century of the RTÉSO was one of positive development and certainly RTÉ's commitment to its musicians had not been misplaced.

3

FROM RTÉSO TO NSO
1973-1998

The second quarter-century of the Orchestra's existence has seen changes as great as the first. Not only has it grown in size and significance, but it has become a subject of even more serious political consideration than in the years of its original establishment. Funding has been one source of discussion, but the role of a national symphony orchestra in relation to its broadcasting functions, and in relation to the source of its employment, has been the focus of intense debate in the past decade. The RTÉ Authority identified this in its inaugural Annual Report in 1960-61 when it pointed out that such an orchestra, with responsibilities beyond those of broadcasting, should be financed from other sources besides those of the broadcasting budget.

Furthermore, the relationship between RTÉ and the Principal Conductor of its Symphony Orchestra has changed over the years, in the course of which difficult decisions have had to be made in the interests of the institution, in order to maintain a clear managerial and artistic policy as well as a vibrant sense of direction in the work of the Orchestra and those on the podium.

Contemporary emphasis continues

Albert Rosen continued to demonstrate the extraordinary breadth and depth of his musical interests and of his musicality itself, being apparently capable of taking on music in every genre, although his métier and his chief love outside the opera house was clearly that of the large-scale romantic school and the music of his native Czechoslovakia. Perhaps the most astonishing example of this was his willingness and ability to step in at a day's notice to replace an indisposed Krzystof Penderecki in performances of his Flute Concerto and Sinfonietta in 1995.

In June 1973 Rosen gave the Irish premiere of Henze's Third Symphony at the SFX, while in January 1974 the brilliant young Korean violinist Kyung Wha Chung made her Dublin début in the Berg Concerto in a 20th Century Festival concert in St Patrick's Training College in Drumcondra. Colman Pearce conducted and introduced Franco Donatoni's *'Puppenspiel* No.1' and Lutoslawski's Second Symphony to Ireland for the first time.

Irish music during the year included Gerald Barry's 'Lessness' (text by Samuel Beckett) on 5 February with Anne Woodworth and Minnie Clancy who also premiered Seoirse Bodley's 'Ceathruintí Mháire Ní Ogáin' (to a text by Máire Mhac an tSaoí) on 7 June. Veronica Dunne, the dedicatee, gave the first performance of the orchestral version of James Wilson's 'Irish Songs' on 30 August, while Conor Farrington was the narrator in the premiere of Frank

24 March 1974
Gaiety Theatre

Berlioz: Damnation of Faust

Jane Manning, soprano
John Mitchinson, tenor
William Young, baritone
Jacques Villisech, bass
Goethe Institute Choir
Choir of St Mary's Haddington Road
RTÉ Choral Society
RTÉ Singers
Albert Rosen, conductor

13 October 1974
Gaiety Theatre

Haydn:	Symphony no 40
Shostakovich:	Piano Concerto no 2
Bruckner:	Symphony no 9

John O'Conor, piano
Albert Rosen, conductor

17 May 1978
St Francis Xavier Hall

Vaughan Williams:	Fantasia on a theme of Thomas Tallis
Grieg:	Piano Concerto
Victory:	Symphony no 2 ('Il ricorso')*

Hugh Tinney, piano
Colman Pearce, conductor
**First public performance*

19 July 1978
St Francis Xavier Hall

John Gibson:	Chamber Music
Elgar:	Violin Concerto
Rachmaninov:	Symphonic Dances

Alan Smale, violin
Colman Pearce, conductor

Colin Staveley

Dubliner Colin Staveley studied at the RIAM and became leader of the British National Youth Orchestra in 1959. He was appointed leader of the RTÉSO at the age of 32, having previously been the youngest leader of a British orchestra, the BBC Welsh Symphony, and co-leader of the RPO.

Corcoran's 'Two Meditations on poems of John Barth' on September 6, and Veronica McSwiney revived AJ Potter's 'Concerto da Chiesa' on September 20.

On 16 February the soloist was the distinguished Czech violinist, Josef Suk, who played the first Martinů Concerto. It had been assumed, by default, that Suk was going to play 'the' Martinů concerto, as only one such was generally known to exist. The music had been ordered and the programme notes, written at that time and indeed for several years by Anthony Quigley, had been compiled. However, the details emanating from Prague alerted Richard Pine (who had succeeded Leo Donnelly as Concerts Manager) to a discrepancy between 'the' concerto and the one Suk was bringing with him - which was in fact an early work, presumed lost and recently rediscovered which Suk, the leading Czech violinist, had introduced in Chicago and Prague and was now giving its first Irish performance. A frantic search for the score ensued, underlining the fact that any concert can be a headache for the orchestra librarian as well as the conductor (in this case Colman Pearce).

The Orchestra made its final visit to the National Stadium on 27 June 1975 for *The Dream of Gerontius* as part of a John Henry Newman celebration and played for *Messiah* in the 150th anniversary programme of Dublin's Pro-Cathedral on 17 and 18 December. Our Lady's Choral Society, under the baton of Alun Francis in both works, had soloists Bernadette Greevy, Alexander Young and William Young in the one and Mary Sheridan, Patricia Dolan, William McKinney and Eric Hinds in the other.

Among the year's international soloists were Henryk Szeryng who played the Mendelssohn Violin Concerto with Colman Pearce on 11 November, and James Galway made one of his rare appearances with the Orchestra on 23 November when he played the Nielsen Concerto with Albert Rosen conducting - a concert that had had to be postponed from the previous year owing to the sudden death of President Erskine Childers. That programme also had a revival of Brian Boydell's 'Symphonic Inscapes'.

In January 1997 Albert Rosen recalled for me with particular delight his involvement with the performance of Olivier Messiaen's *Turangalîla-symphonie* in the composer's presence at the SFX Hall on 10 January 1976. This was part of that year's 20th Century Festival and the composer's visit had come through the cultural section of the French Embassy. This was another splendid musical affair with Yvonne Loriod (Madame Messiaen) and her sister Jeanne Loriod as soloists, helping to lift the usually mundane appearance of the SFX Hall, which was packed to capacity for the occasion. The work and composer had an ecstatic reception.

First European tour

But there were further circumstances of that order in 1976 as Albert Rosen took the Orchestra on tour to seven English and Welsh destinations and then ventured for the first time to mainland Europe with concerts in Antwerp, Kleve and Rotterdam.

1976 TOUR

Bristol – Colston Hall	12 March
Leeds – Town Hall	13 March
Manchester – Free Trade Hall	14 March
Newcastle-upon-Tyne – City Hall	16 March
Cardiff – Barry – Memorial Hall	18 March
Huddersfield – Town Hall	19 March
Croydon – Fairfield Halls	21 March
Antwerp – Salle Reine Elisabeth	24/25 March
Kleve – Stadthalle	27 March
Rotterdam – De Doelen	28 March

Tour Manager: Richard Pine

Works:	Frederick May	Sunlight and Shadow
	Weber:	Overture, *Euryanthe*
	Richard Strauss:	'Don Juan'
	Elgar:	Sea Pictures
	Beethoven:	Piano Concerto no 1
	Beethoven:	Piano Concerto no 3
	Tchaikovsky:	Variations on a Rococo Theme
	Mahler:	Symphony no 1
	Berlioz:	Symphonie fantastique
	Dvořák:	Symphony no 9

Artists: Bernadette Greevy, contralto
John O'Conor, piano
John Lill, piano
Moura Lympany, piano
André Navarra, cello

Leader: Colin Staveley

Conductor: Albert Rosen

This was the first foray by the Orchestra into the heartland of the musical world from which its repertoire was largely drawn, and it was considered essential that the players should be able to experience the *frisson* to be gained from performing to audiences other than the familiar 'home supporters' - audiences who were well used to visiting orchestras as well as very fine resident bands. To experience a Dutch or German audience giving unstinted applause is now something with which the members of the NSO are familiar, and has fully justified financial and managerial resources required to make it possible.

Reception by foreign audiences was so warm, in fact, that the following year the Orchestra made a short sortie to Germany in March with Albert Rosen to give a single concert in the Rheingoldhalle in Mainz as part of a regular series of visiting orchestras. John O'Conor was the soloist in Beethoven's Third Piano Concerto which had Tchaikovsky's Fourth as its symphonic coupling and Britten's 'Purcell Variations and Fugue' to begin.

Meanwhile in 1976 the Orchestra celebrated the Bicentenary of the United States with a special Gaiety concert on 4 July 1976. Colman Pearce conducted Roy Harris's Third Symphony, with Cristina Ortiz playing the Gershwin Piano Concerto. Celebrating fifty years of Irish Broadcasting in 1976, RTÉ commissioned Brian Boydell to compose 'Jubilee Music', premiered at the Gaiety on 3 October. The composer dedicated the work to the Orchestra 'whose service to Irish music over the years has been inestimable'. The piece incorporated a 'somewhat distorted fragment of "O'Donnell Abú" - Radio Éireann's call sign - while the jig "Patsy Mack" recorded the Station's commitment to Irish traditional music'.

In Wexford the following year, 1977, a small element of history was made. Jane Glover became the first woman to direct the Orchestra in public when she conducted the Festival production of Gluck's *Orfeo ed Euridice*. Albert Rosen led the DGOS in Massenet's *Werther* and Napoleone Annovazzi undertook the first Irish performances of the Paris version of Wagner's *Tannhäuser*.

1978 saw another 20th Century Festival during which the renowned Witold Lutoslawski was the Orchestra's conductor at the SFX Hall on 13 January. His programme included his First Symphony and Cello Concerto with the brilliant young Austrian artist, Heinrich Schiff - again, it was one of those occasions which stay in the minds of those who witnessed not only a fine individual performance but also the emergence of a new talent - in this case Schiff - as well as a partnership between Lutoslawski and Schiff, who became his chosen interpreter. The Festival's opening concert on 6 January, dedicated to Irish composers, included Fleischmann's 'Sinfonia Votiva', Potter's 'Sinfonia De Profundis' and James Wilson's settings of W B Yeats, 'A Woman Young and Old', with soprano Jane Manning.

A novel element was also attached to a Trinity College concert on 5 May when Seán Cahill, the Orchestra's principal trombone, was heard in the Czech composer Josef Matej's First Concerto with Proinnsías Ó Duinn and the following month St Michael's Church in Dun Laoghaire, which houses a fascinating Dutch Rieger organ, was the

11 March 1979
Gaiety Theatre

Respighi: Rossiniana
Gerard Schurmann: Violin Concerto
Mussorgsky/Ravel: Pictures at an Exhibition

Ruggiero Ricci, violin
Albert Rosen, conductor
This concert was repeated in the City Hall, Cork, on 12 March

16 June 1979
RDS
Festival of Music and Musicians

Brahms: Academic Festival Overture
Brahms: Concerto for violin and cello
Richard Strauss: Don Quixote

Paul Tortelier, cello
Constantin Zanidache, viola
Jan Pascal Tortelier, violin/conductor

27 July 1979
St Francis Xavier Hall
Gala concert of symphonic jazz

Seiber: Improvisations for jazz band and orchestra
Shaeffer: Concerto for jazz ensemble and symphony orchestra
Liebermann: Concerto for jazz ensemble and symphony orchestra
Gershwin: Rhapsody in Blue
Gershwin: Eight Songs (arr. Laurie Holloway)

Philip Martin, piano
Marian Montgomery, vocalist
Colman Pearce, conductor

16 June 1982
NCH
Stravinsky Centenary Concert

Jeu de Cartes
Huxley Variations
Capriccio
Symphony in three movements

Mićeál O'Rourke, piano
Colman Pearce, conductor

Orchestra's unusual venue when Gerard Gillen was Ó Duinn's soloist in Poulenc's Concerto. Back in the SFX Hall there were some visiting conductors. Fritz Maraffi directed Philip Martin through the 'Burleske' of Richard Strauss and the first performance of his own 'Terpsichore' on 5 July while the Norwegian Per Dreier guided Pádraig O'Rourke across the pitfalls of Frank Martin's 'Jedermann Monologues' on 12 July. Following the summer recess Colin Staveley played Andrzej Panufnik's Violin Concerto on 6 September which Colman Pearce, who had a singular affinity with the composer's music, conducted. The following week, Lynda Byrne, who would, in time, become the Orchestra's pianist and celeste player, was the soloist in the Shostakovich First Concerto. Pierre Michel le Conte conducted and chose Dvořák's 'New World' Symphony as his main work.

Albert Rosen remembered the fiftieth anniversary of Janáček's death with a concert in St Patrick's Cathedral on 22 September with the Sinfonietta and *Glagolitic Mass*. It was the Guinness Choir's turn here with Janet Price, Anne Woodworth, John Mitchinson, Jaroslav Horáček and Gerard Gillen.

Appointment of a co-leader

The young English violinist Alan Smale had become the RTÉSO's co-leader with Colin Staveley in 1977. In 1978 Catherine Smale and Raymond Griffiths had joined the first violins; Carlos Assa-Munt and Claire Crehan were in the seconds. Elizabeth Csibi and Thomas Kane were listed in the viola section. Aisling Drury Byrne had become Principal Cello with Dairíne Ní Mheadhra among the rank and file. She would later form and conduct the contemporary music group Nua Nós before emigrating to Canada in the 1990s.

In the winds, Madeleine Berkeley and Deirdre Brady were in the flutes, with David Carmody and Colin Block among the horns. Martin Metrustry was the timpanist and a Polish musician, Michael Czerwinski was leading the percussion players.

Colin Staveley resigned his leadership during the first quarter of 1979 and was succeeded by Audrey Park, who had been leader of the Concert Orchestra and, before that, of the RTÉ String Quartet. Audrey Park was a striking figure who brought an air of fashion as well as extraordinary musicianship to her position. It seemed particularly fitting that two of her initial concerts focused on violin concertos. Erich Gruenberg played the Britten at the SFX Hall on 19 September with Albert Rosen, who also conducted Ralph Holmes in the Harty Concerto at the Gaiety on 7 October.

1980, Albert Rosen's last year as Principal Conductor, opened with Colman Pearce at the 20th Century Festival at the SFX Hall. Brian O'Rourke and John Finucane were the soloists in Durkó's Second Clarinet Rhapsody; and Elliott Carter, in Dublin for the event, heard the first Irish performance of his own Variations for Orchestra. Pierre Michel le Conte conducted the first Irish performance of Dutilleux's *'Métaboles'* on 9 January with the husband and wife duo of Howard Shelley and Hilary MacNamara playing Poulenc's Concerto for Two Pianos.

1980 TOUR

Edinburgh – Usher Hall	4 March
Leeds – Town Hall	5 March
Hanley, Stoke-on-Trent – Victoria Hall	7 March
Birmingham – Town Hall	8 March
London – Royal Festival Hall	10 March
Antwerp – Salle Reine Elisabeth	12/13 March
Paris – Salle Pleyel	14 March
Paris – Salle Gaveau	15 March
Strasbourg – Palais des Fêtes	17 March
Neustadt-an-der-Weinstrasse – Stadt Saalban	18 March
Stuttgart – Böblingen – Kongresshalle	20 March
Koblenz – Rheinmoselhalle	21 March
Bielefeld – Oetkerhalle	22 March

Tour Manager: Richard Pine

Works:	Brian Boydell:	In Memoriam Mahatma Gandhi
	A J Potter:	Rhapsody under a High Sky
	Gerard Victory:	Olympic Festival Overture
	Janáček:	Taras Bulba
	Rossini:	Overture, 'La gazza ladra'
	Barber:	Piano Concerto
	Beethoven:	Piano Concerto no 3
	Beethoven:	Piano Concerto no 4
	Chausson:	Poème
	Elgar:	Sea Pictures
	Gershwin:	Piano Concerto
	Mahler:	*Lieder eines fahrenden Gesellen*
	Rachmaninov:	Piano Concerto no 3
	Ravel:	Tzigane
	Wagner:	Wesendonck lieder
	Brahms:	Symphony no 1
	Dvořák:	Symphony no 8
	Dvořák:	Symphony no 9
	Mahler:	Symphony no 5
	Tchaikovsky:	Symphony no 5
	Chabrier:	España
	Falla:	Dances from 'Three Cornered Hat'

Artists: Bernadette Greevy, contralto
Philip Martin, piano
John O'Conor, piano
Geraldine O'Grady, violin
Mićeál O'Rourke, piano

Leader: Audrey Park
Conductors: Albert Rosen, Colman Pearce

European Tour – 1980

On 26 and 27 February Rosen and Pearce previewed some of the programme for the Orchestra's latest and longest tour abroad up to that time, which would see the Orchestra revisiting Antwerp, where it had enjoyed a particular success in 1976, as well as Paris, Strasbourg and Stuttgart. It was once again a striking artistic success, contributing hugely to the self-confidence and self-esteem of the players and their supporting personnel.

A move from base of a different order occurred in July 1980, and saw the Orchestra participating in yet another fresh initiative. The singular setting was the Church of the Annunciation in Dublin's Finglas West; the occasion, the first Dublin International Organ Festival. The church's organ had been originally built in 1869 in All Saints, Sydenham, London and having been dismantled was brought to Dublin and re-erected in Finglas in 1979 by the firm of Grant, Degens and Bradbeer. The soloist was Desmond Hunter in Joseph Jongen's Symphonie Concertante (1926) and the Third (Organ) Symphony of Saint-Saëns. The concert opened suitably with Panufnik's purely orchestral 'Concerto Festivo'. Four years later the same Festival would find the Orchestra at the Carmelite Church in Dublin's Whitefriar Street. Peter Hurford was the soloist in the Poulenc Concerto under Eimear Ó Broin to inaugurate the church's new Kenneth Jones instrument.

Further curiosity came on 17 September 1980 at the SFX Hall, when Michael Berkofsky and John O'Conor gave the first Irish performance, under Colman Pearce, of a recently discovered Two-Piano Concerto by Max Bruch.

Albert Rosen gave his last concert as Principal Conductor at the Gaiety on 23 November in a programme which suited him admirably - Richard Strauss's 'Till Eulenspiegel' and 'Don Quixote', with Archie Collins and Aisling Drury Byrne, and Stravinsky's Firebird Suite. Rosen went on to conduct four excellent performances of Beethoven's *Fidelio* for the DGOS, once again showing himself to be a man of diverse musical resources.

Colman Pearce as Principal Conductor

Colman Pearce took over the RTÉSO from January 1981. He had had a long association with Radio Éireann, joining first in 1961 as music scriptwriter. He had become Tibor Paul's assistant in 1965 and Pearce's first concert with the RTÉSO was on 5 March that year at the Metropolitan Hall, when his initial programme had comprised the Reznicek *Donna Diana* Overture, Dvořák's Symphonic Variations, Weber's First Clarinet Concerto (Richard West, the RTÉSO's principal at the time) and the Sibelius Second Symphony. Pearce took over the Gaiety concert on 16 October 1966 following Tibor Paul's heart attack and soon established himself as a formidable figure in Ireland's music-making. His programme then was Stravinsky's Firebird Suite, Prokofiev's First Violin Concerto with Josef Sivo, and Beethoven's Fifth Symphony. He enjoyed enormous support from Gerard Victory and had considerable freedom to advance his career abroad. Colman Pearce was appointed Co-principal with Albert Rosen for the years 1978-1980.

1981 was also a crucial year for RTÉ's involvement in music in Dublin as the

Gerard Larner in *The Guardian* on the Stoke-on-Trent concert of 6 March

"As well as being a precise and vigorous ensemble, it seemed in the first half to be one with an attractive and well balanced overall sound....In Elgar's Sea Pictures there were some lovely orchestral sounds...to accompany Bernadette Greevy's resourceful and luxuriously coloured singing....In the Brahms it was the strength of the string section and the firmness of trumpets and trombones which, together with Rosen's well calculated interpretation, made the favourable impression".

Barry Grayson in *The Birmingham Post* on the Birmingham concert on 8 March

"The orchestra has personality, with every department of it, particularly the strings section, displaying virtuosity within a sure ensemble framework, and its playing, always colourful, held flexibility as well as artistic success....maybe it (Taras Bulba) succeeded, but here it impressed as a piece of heroic melodrama with Rosen building tension to a high pitch of excitement....John O'Conor is a Beethoven pianist of distinction and his playing.... developed a sense of spontaneity and expressive poetry that remained completely unmannered....Above all, the power of the finale (Dvořak's Eighth) added effectiveness to a reading of formidable musical stature".

William Mann in *The Times* after the Royal Festival Hall concert on 10 March (which was part of the Sense of Ireland Festival, a wide ranging showcase of Irish arts in London during February and March 1980)

"The RTÉ Symphony Orchestra's present standard is high....The brass choir excels, precise and resplendent and dauntless ; the woodwinds are nicely blended, with sensitive soloists (the principal flute perhaps specially winning in tone and musicality), the strings eminently capable....Their leader, Audrey Park, is extremely able, and handsome to look at...In the Tchaikovsky Mr Pearce paid exemplary attention to matters of nuance throughout, and was generously rewarded. The music emerged with welcome freshness and impact".

Felix Aprahamian in *The Sunday Times* on the same concert

"Tchaikovsky's Fifth revealed fine discipline as well as clear, colourful woodwind timbres of the kind that give an orchestra its own particular physiognomy".

De Standaard, Antwerp, on the concert there on 13 March

"The Irish pianist Míceál O'Rourke can be considered as being among the best interpreters of the moment, judging by the sensitive, lively expression which he gave to Rachmaninov's Third Piano Concerto. Touch, nuance and phrasing are of excellent quality".

Gazet van Antwerpen on the same concert

"It is a solid and accomplished ensemble of strength in which the transparent violin tone, the sonorous quality of the horns, clarinet and bassoon deserve special mention. A presence which in addition was directed by Colman Pearce with outstanding rhythmic and interpretative authority".

Brigitte Massin of *Le Matin de Paris* on the first Paris concert on 14 March

"Mahler's Fifth....confirmed the excellent ensemble of the orchestra and the quality of its section leaders especially of violins, horns and cellos. The novelty of Mahler's orchestration which is so specifically evident in this symphony was shown off splendidly".

eagerly awaited National Concert Hall was coming to fruition. The Government had long since decided against pursuing the originally planned site at Beggar's Bush and the matter hung in the balance for quite some time. The transfer of University College, Dublin, to new premises at Belfield, left space in the old building in Earlsfort Terrace. The conversion of its Examination Hall into the National Concert Hall was begun in the late 1970s (by the Office of Public Works, where the architect in charge was Michael O'Doherty, husband of Moya O'Grady, a member of the cello section of the Orchestra), with the opening planned for September 1981. However, to be viable, the Hall would need the presence of the RTÉSO.

There was no doubt in the mind of the RTÉ Authority that the transfer of the Orchestra's home from the SFX, and the creation of the NCH as the centre of its orchestral music-making, was essential, even though it would incur a substantial increase in costs. For the RTÉSO's devotees at the SFX, of course, the move would mean an alteration to the pattern of their concert going. There was free entry to the SFX Hall, which was extremely advantageous to many elderly members of the local community, but this would cease with the transfer. On the other side of the coin the prestigious nature of the new hall would surely bring in its own clientèle. From the musicians' point of view the change of venue could only bring many advantages, one of which was more convenient and comfortable back-stage facilities, and another the almost complete cessation of Saturday rehearsals and Sunday night concerts which the use of the Gaiety for the Subscription series had necessitated - from now on, the regular concert night would be Friday.

But the Orchestra spent the first half of 1981 at the SFX, largely due to the fact that it had not been possible to obtain a firm completion date for the NCH. Furthermore, concert programmes and soloists, planned by the Director of Music, the Principal Conductor and the guest conductors, are scheduled approximately 24 months in advance, in order to secure the services of the best and most appropriate artists on the international concert circuit, and it therefore proved impossible to abandon the Sunday night arrangement until after the move to the NCH had been made.

The first concert of 1981, however, was at the RDS, where Colman Pearce conducted the premiere of Seoirse Bodley's Second Symphony. Subtitled 'I have loved the lands of Ireland', commissioned by the Government for the Pádraig Pearse centenary. Veronica McSwiney played John Field's Second Piano Concerto. The Orchestra returned to the RDS on 29 September 1981 to mark the Society's 250th anniversary with a concert featuring Mićeál O'Rourke playing Rachmaninov's Third Concerto. Albert Rosen conducted, with Mahler's First Symphony after the interval.

Eimear Ó Broin was at the Gaiety on 22 February when the English soprano Sheila Armstrong was heard in the 'Four Last Songs' of Richard Strauss. John Beckett, better known in the music of Bach, went to the other end of the musical spectrum by undertaking Deryck Cooke's performing version of Mahler's Tenth Symphony at the SFX Hall on 27 March. A performance of Bartók's Dance

Marie-Rose Clouzot in *Activités Musicales* on the same concert

"I should add also that the leader - Audrey Park - has a superb sound and that the conductor - Albert Rosen - conducts with as much enthusiasm as precision....I stress solely that the individual quality of the orchestral players (about one-third of whom are women) brought the work *(Mahler's Fifth)* to a very high level".

Dernières Nouvelles D'Alsace on the first Strasbourg concert on 17 March

"The excellent violinist Geraldine O'Grady....succeeded admirably in....the passionate, rhapsodic song of Chausson's Poème and was no less successful in the solo part of Ravel's Tzigane a part stuffed with so many virtuoso 'tours de force'. A richly rewarding evening".

Ulrich Bumann in the *Rhein-Zeitung* after the Koblenz concert on 21 March

"And the Irish brought along a 'natural' for the piano , Philip Martin... His hammering out of Barber's highly complicated score was a true joy".

And from the *Westfalen Blatt* after the Bielefeld concert on 22 March

"The perfection of playing and the high level of the conductor (Albert Rosen) ensured a flexibly moulded performance throughout this so frequently played symphony *(Brahms's First)*. The value of such a performance, however, lies in this that it made a decisive step beyond the perfection of a recording towards a living interpretation. The public were correspondingly delighted".

30 June 1982
NCH
Haydn 250th anniversary
Part of the Dublin International Organ Festival

Symphony no 28
Organ Concertos nos 1 and 2
Creation Mass

Gerard Gillen, organ
Virginia Kerr, soprano
Anna Caleb, contralto
Frank Dunne, tenor
Pádraig O'Rourke, bass
St James's Choir
Colman Pearce, conductor

25 May 1983
NCH

Mendelssohn: 'Hebrides' overture
Sibelius: Violin Concerto
Beethoven: Symphony no 4

Pierre Amoyal, violin
Okko Kamu, conductor

11 May 1983
NCH

Walton: Overture, 'Portsmouth Point'
Chopin: Piano Concerto no 2
Sibelius: Symphony no 5

Hugh Tinney, piano
Bryden Thomson, conductor

18 May 1983
NCH

May: Spring Nocturne
Mozart: Concerto for two pianos, K365
Walton: Symphony no 1

Howard Shelley and Hilary Macnamara, pianos
Bryden Thomson, conductor

1 June 1983
NCH

Weber: Overture, 'Oberon'
Sallinen: Cello Concerto
Prokofiev: Symphony no 5

Aisling Drury Byrne, cello
Bryden Thomson, conductor

Suite in the Hall on 24 June was halted by Colman Pearce when a dog in one of the aisles decided it was all too much. An attendant removed the offending hound. Nothing of this kind had occurred in recent years, although on one Sunday at the Gaiety a baby elephant, caged at the back of the theatre during the winter pantomime, added its trumpet tones to those of the horns in a performance of Bruckner's Third Symphony. The only other occasion at the SFX when anything went awry was in the 1970s when an enthusiast, disgruntled at being excluded from a full house, smashed the plate glass doors of the hall in an effort to hear Vincenzo Caminiti's performance of the Elgar Cello Concerto.

But the days of the Orchestra's 'temporary' sojourn in the St Francis Xavier Hall were coming to an end. Colman Pearce took the final concert on 29 July. The Hungarian pianist Zoltán Kocsis played Bartók's Third Concerto after John Buckley's ballet suite 'Fornacht do Chonac Thú'. Farewells were said with Elgar's Enigma Variations. The Hall was full but few seemed to mourn. The musicians went on holiday and a new era was about to begin.

National Concert Hall

The State opening of the National Concert Hall by the President, Dr Patrick Hillery, on 9 September 1981 was a glittering occasion. It was fitting that Colman Pearce, the first Irishman to hold the official position of Principal Conductor, was on the rostrum for the premiere of Seoirse Bodley's RTÉ-commissioned Third Symphony, *Ceol,* which called for large vocal and orchestral forces. Its text, by Brendan Kennelly, was sung by Violet Twomey, Bernadette Greevy, Louis Browne, William Young, the RTÉ Singers, Chorus, Our Lady's Choral Society and Boys of St Patrick's Cathedral Choir, with introduction to each movement spoken by Aindreas Ó Gallchoir. Beethoven's Ninth Symphony followed and the concert was repeated for the general public the following evening.

The first manager of the Hall was Lindsay Armstrong, a former oboe and cor anglais player in the RTÉSO who had become Manager of the New Irish Chamber Orchestra, and his secretary was Anne Cant, who had appeared as soprano soloist with the Orchestra on several occasions. The first Board of Directors included RTÉ Director of Music, Gerard Victory, Veronica Dunne, Bernadette Greevy, Seoirse Bodley and Colonel Fred O'Callaghan, who were appointed by An Taoiseach, Charles J Haughey.

Maestro Rosen made his National Concert Hall début on 4 October with Bruckner's Sixth Symphony and Martino Tirimo playing Rachmaninov's Paganini Rhapsody.

One of the earliest events - or 'non-events' as it turned out - in the new hall was a concert in the 20th Century Festival in January 1982 which brought the controversial figure of Karlheinz Stockhausen to Dublin. His orchestral 'Inori' was one of the works planned. Freak weather conditions prevailed during that week and some musicians were unable to reach the NCH in time for the start of rehearsals. The composer grew uneasy, and heated verbal exchanges followed between him and some of the artists. In the heel of the

Colman Pearce

Dublin-born Colman Pearce took an Honours Music Degree at UCD and won many awards as a pianist before studying conducting in Vienna with Hans Swarovsky. He was Principal Conductor of the RTÉSO 1981-83, and Principal Guest Conductor with the Bilbao Symphony 1984-87. Since 1987 he has been Principal Conductor and Music Director of the Mississippi Symphony, in addition to which he makes frequent guest appearances. He is particularly noted for directing the premieres of many Irish works, in addition to introducing much contemporary music to Irish audiences at the 'Summer Music at Carrolls' series during the 1970s and 1980s. On CD he has conducted works by Stanford, Victory *(Ultima Rerum)* and Boydell.

Audrey Park

hunt, the orchestral involvement was cancelled even though the hall was fully subscribed, and Stockhausen introduced the performance from a commercial recording with the participation of dance soloists before returning home.

Matters settled down after that in time for everyone to revel in the 'Alpine' Symphony of Richard Strauss under Albert Rosen, and the following week (29 January) George Hurst conducted the Orchestra in Walton's Viola Concerto with the eminent Walter Trampler. A special James Joyce centenary concert on 5 February found Anna Manahan reciting the lines from *Finnegans Wake* in a repeat of Humphrey Searle's 'Riverrun'. Gerard Victory's 'Six Epiphanies of an Author' was the composer's homage to Joyce.

The American, Victoria Bond, took the baton on 7 July to conduct her own 'Equinox' and Rachmaninov's Second Symphony. Colman Pearce gave the first performance here of Peter Maxwell Davies's Second Symphony on 15 September, and the Tippett Piano Concerto resurfaced with Paul Crossley and Eimear Ó Broin on 22 September.

The year ended with 'The Music Festival to end all Music Festivals'. Some very unusual characters acted as the 'Mixed Soloists' in James Wilson's 'Umbrage'. This New Year's Eve fun piece had the critics Fanny Feehan, Mary MacGoris, Ian Fox, John Honohan, James Maguire and myself in various occupations, aided and abetted by the RTÉSO. Some of us accused the conductor, Proinnsías Ó Duinn, of taking quiet revenge. In the same event John O'Conor played a typewriter in a piece by Brian Boydell, and Philip Martin, Franz Reizenstein's 'Concerto Popolare'. (Reizenstein had been one of Martin's teachers in London.) Mary Sheridan was Carmel in 'Ceoldráma le Seoirse Bizet'. The 'concert' was also televised live in Anne Makower's production.

1984 began with another of the Music Association's 20th Century Festivals. Noel Eccles, then the vibrant leader of the percussion section, premiered Noel Kelehan's 'Three Pieces for Percussion and Orchestra', and Mary Sheridan was involved in Stravinsky's rarely heard *Persephone,* with tenor Nigel Robson, and the Dublin County and Palestrina Choirs. Albert Rosen was in charge and, with cellists, Aage Kvalbein, introduced two works - 'Epitaffio' and 'Tenebrae' - by Arne Nordheim.

Later that year Colman Pearce premiered Gerard Victory's epic *Ultima Rerum.* With its texts drawn from many sources, it showed the genius of the composer's inspiration in an extraordinary manner. The soloists were Virginia Kerr, Bernadette Greevy, Adrian Thompson and Peter McBrien, with the Guinness and Palestrina Choirs. The work captured the imagination of its audience, as it has been revived several times since, and was recorded by the NSO in the Naxos Irish Composers' Series.

The summer of 1984 brought a trial set of Tuesday one-hour lunchtime concerts to the NCH. The success of the initial series has shown little sign of diminishing. Using mainly younger soloists and including many short works difficult to slot into an evening programme, these concerts bring a particular repertoire not otherwise available to the Orchestra. It

Bryden Thomson

In the course of his career, Bryden Thomson was Principal Conductor of five major orchestras: the BBC Philharmonic, the BBC Welsh, the Ulster Orchestra, the RTÉ/NSO, and lastly the Royal Scottish National Orchestra. He was also closely associated with the Royal Ballet and the Norwegian Opera, and recorded the works of Irish composers extensively with the Ulster Orchestra, which earned him an honorary doctorate from the New University of Ulster.

has also succeeded in adding a new dimension to the working day of many whose offices are in the environs of the NCH.

1984 also saw the departure of Gerard Victory as Director of Music as he wished to devote himself to composition. He was replaced by John Kinsella, with the title Head of Music. Mr Kinsella had been Assistant Head of Music from 1972 and, like Dr Victory, was a well-established composer, having been awarded the Marten Toonder Award for composition by the Arts Council in 1979. He would remain in his post until 1989 and then, himself taking early retirement, dedicate himself to composition. Following in the footsteps of Gerard Victory, he was appointed to the Board of the National Concert Hall in 1991.

Bryden Thomson

Bryden Thomson began to appear more frequently on the rostrum. In one of the first concerts of 1985, Thomson launched into his cycle of Nielsen's music with the Violin Concerto played by Arve Tellefsen. The 'Inextinguishable' Symphony came in February and the rest of the Danish master's output throughout the course of the year.

Bryden Thomson was something of a charismatic figure and even before taking up office as Principal Conductor had become extremely popular with the NCH audiences. As a result his concerts were in the main played to capacity attendances. There was also a strong classical and romantic bent to his programme planning and indeed his first year with the Orchestra included a strong flavour of Dvořák and Tchaikovsky. Both figured for example on 5 July with Ruggiero Ricci returning for Tchaikovsky's Violin Concerto, although the Symphony was Nielsen's First.

He soon launched into another of his favourite cycles, this time featuring Mozart Piano Concertos and Bruckner Symphonies. Like the previous Nielsen sequence it proved extremely worthwhile. Among the concerto pianists were Paul Badura-Skoda, Boris Berman, Walter Klien, Florence Ryan, making a welcome return, and Howard Shelley.

In the orchestral ranks, Timothy Kirwan was listed as deputy leader to Audrey Park, with Catherine and Helen Briscoe, Anna Kane and Sunniva Fitzpatrick also among the first violins. Michael McKenna, Keith Packer and Annemauraid Hamilton were in the seconds and Margaret and John Adams in the violas. David James and Sharon Nye were in the cello section and William McGlynn in the double-basses. William Dowdall led the flute section, with Patricia Harrison among the oboes. Lesley Bishop, Fergus O'Carroll and Fergal Ó Ceallacháin were in the horns.

On 16 July Colman Pearce, who was now RTÉ's Senior Staff Conductor, introduced three new Irish works, Raymond Deane's *'Enchaînement'*, Gerard Victory's Third Symphony and a Cello Concerto by James Wilson with Aisling Drury Byrne. The Belfast pianist, Barry Douglas, then on the threshold of his career, opened the 1986 Festival of 20th Century Music with Bartók's Third Concerto. Bryden Thomson was on the rostrum to premiere Jerome de Bromhead's First Symphony. The second Festival concert on 11 January

29 June 1983
NCH

Brahms: Tragic Overture
Ives: The Unanswered Question
Haydn: Cello Concerto in C
Potter: Symphony no 2 ('Ireland')*

Florian Kitt, cello
Robert Gutter, conductor
**First Irish performance*

18 July 1986
NCH

Franck: Le Chasseur maudit
Frank Martin: Petite Symphonie Concertante
Beethoven: Symphony no 7

Denise Kelly, harp
John O'Sullivan, harpsichord
Lynda Byrne, piano
Jean Meylan, conductor

1 August 1986
NCH
Liszt centenary

Mazeppa
Piano Concerto no 2
Dante Symphony

Veronica McSwiney, piano
RTÉ Chorus
Albert Rosen, conductor

26 September 1986
NCH

Delius: Sea Drift
Janáček: Suite from 'The House of the Dead'
Rachmaninov: The Bells

Mary Sheridan de Bruin, soprano
Louis Browne, tenor,
Pádraig O'Rourke, bass
Guinness Choir
Albert Rosen, conductor

19 November 1986
NCH

Ó Riada: The Banks of Sullane
Rachmaninov: Piano Concerto no 4
Dvořák: Symphony no 7

Peter Donohoe, piano
Bryden Thomson, conductor
This concert was also performed in Cork (20th) and Waterford (21st)

3 April 1987
NCH

Bach: Orchestral Suite no 3
Berg: Violin Concerto
Schumann: Symphony no 4

Gyorgy Pauk, violin
János Fürst, conductor

10 April 1987
NCH

Mendelssohn: Elijah

Teresa Cahill, soprano
Bernadette Greevy, contralto
Philip Langridge, tenor
Wolfgang Schöne, bass
RTÉ Philharmonic Choir
Dublin Boy Singers
János Fürst, conductor

20 February 1987
NCH

Ravel: Suite, Ma mère l'oye
Ravel: Shéhérazade*
Sibelius: Tapiola
Shostakovich: Symphony no 6

Mary Sheridan de Bruin, soprano
Eimear Ó Broin, conductor
**Commemorating the 50th anniversary of Ravel's death*

was devoted in the main to the music of György Ligeti. His 'Lontano', 'Melodien', and Flute and Oboe Concerto (the visiting Sebastian Bell and Gareth Hulse) were conducted by Elgar Howarth.

The Dublin International Organ Festival took the Orchestra to St Patrick's Cathedral on 27 June for Britten's *War Requiem* with the RTÉ Philharmonic Choir, trained by Colin Mawby, making one of its first public appearances with the boys of the Cathedral and Palestrina Choirs. The soloists this time round with Colman Pearce were Jennifer Smith, Maldwyn Davies and Peter McBrien.

At this time it once again became a feature of artistic policy to showcase the talents of the orchestra players (particularly section leaders) as concerto soloists. Matthew Manning, for example, played Mozart's Oboe Concerto with Albert Rosen on 31 July, and Alan Smale, Walton's Violin Concerto with Bryden Thomson on 9 October. Earlier, on 5 June, Deirdre Brady and Helen Davies, who was then the RTÉ Concert Orchestra's harpist, had been the soloists in Mozart's Flute and Harp Concerto with Colman Pearce. Since then several concertos have been specially commissioned by RTÉ for section leaders of the NSO, including one by Raymond Deane for Matthew Manning, and another by Philip Martin for Andreja Malíř.

At the same time, the presentation of Irish works continued vigorously: among them were Gerald Barry's 'Of Queen's Gardens' (János Fürst); a reprise of John Buckley's 'Fornacht do Chonac Thú' (Albert Rosen) at the NCH and in Cork; Frank Corcoran's 'Symphonies of Symphonies for Wind' (János Fürst); Brian Boydell's 'Symphonic Inscapes' (János Fürst); and the premiere of Raymond Deane's commissioned 'Thresholds' (Proinnsías Ó Duinn), on New Year's Eve to celebrate the arrival of Dublin's Millennium.

Appointment of János Fürst

Disagreements between himself and John Kinsella led to a decision by RTÉ not to extend Bryden Thomson's contract beyond 1987. In his place, RTÉ appointed János Fürst, who had been a violinist in the Orchestra in the late 1950s and had since developed a career as a conductor. His particular skill as a string specialist was regarded as necessary at that time to strengthen this side of the Orchestra's development. However, Fürst's relationship with the Orchestra deteriorated during his first year as Principal Conductor, and in mid-1989 he asked to be released from the remainder of his contract. This resignation marked a deepening of RTÉ's problems, in identifying the appropriate artistic personnel to entrust with the Orchestra's development, which were to last until the appointment of Kasper de Roo in 1994.

Fürst's initial concert on 8 January 1988 was devoted to Mahler's Second Symphony with Sheila Armstrong, Bernadette Greevy and the RTÉ Philharmonic Choir and his plan was to continue the cycle of Mahler's orchestral works during his term of office. Fürst almost achieved his goal, with only the Eighth eluding him due to the enormous forces required. This colossus would manifest itself in other circumstances after his departure.

26 April 1987
NCH
Ó Riada retrospective

Olynthiac Overture
Nomos 4*
Nomos 2**

John O'Conor, piano*
Jack O'Kelly, baritone**
Dublin County Choir
Bryden Thomson, conductor
Cyril Cusack read Séamus Heaney's 'In Memoriam Seán Ó Riada' and John Montague read his 'Ó Riada's Farewell'

Seán Ó Riada

22 May 1987
NCH

Rossini: Overture, 'Semiramide'
Gerald Barry: Of Queen's Gardens
Rachmaninov: Rhapsody on a theme of Paganini
Richard Strauss: Ein Heldenleben

John Gibson, piano
János Fürst, conductor

26 May 1987
NCH (lunchtime)

Beethoven: Overture, 'Egmont'
McNulty: Divertimento
Ravel: Tzigane
Dvořák: Czech Suite

Geraldine O'Grady, violin
János Fürst, conductor

29 May 1987
NCH

Szöllösy: Transfigurations*
Prokofiev: Piano Concerto no 3
Mahler: Symphony no 4

Philip Martin, piano
Mary Hegarty, soprano
János Fürst, conductor
**First Irish performance*

11 September 1987
NCH

Mozart: Symphony no 38, K304
Wagner: *Die Walküre* Act 1

Penelope Daner, soprano
Wolfgang Neumann, tenor
Victor von Halem, bass
János Fürst, conductor

18 September 1987
NCH

Haydn: Symphony no 100 ('Military')
Bartók: Viola Concerto
Schumann: Symphony no 1

Nobuko Imai, viola
János Fürst, conductor

25 September 1987
NCH

Bach: Cantata no 51 ('Jauchzet Gott in allen Landen')
Mahler: Symphony no 6
Virginia Kerr, soprano
János Fürst, conductor

Fürst's second concert included Schoenberg's *'Verklärte Nacht'* and this was soon followed by a rare Irish performance of the composer's Violin Concerto with Pierre Amoyal. Mahler's Seventh Symphony stood alone on 4 March.

Immediately on the heels of the DGOS Spring Season, in which Fürst conducted *Don Giovanni* and Albert Rosen was involved with *Tosca,* the Principal Conductor bravely turned to Richard Strauss and the first Irish performance of his opera *Elektra.* Although in a concert version on 29 April, it was still an historical occasion for the Orchestra. The cast included Anna Green in the title role, with Nuala Willis as Klytemnestra, Carmen Reppel as Chrysosthemis, Kenneth Woollam as Aegisthus and Philip Joll as Orestes.

In September Fürst returned to opera in concert form with Bartók's *Duke Bluebeard's Castle* (Livia Budal and Laszlo Polgar). He then directed the Irish premiere of Lutoslawski's 'Chain 2' (György Pauk), and returned to Mahler with the *Kindertotenlieder* (Bernadette Greevy) and Fifth Symphony.

Colman Pearce made a number of notable appearances with the Orchestra in 1988 as well. He revived Gerard Victory's *Ultima Rerum* and confirmed its extraordinary vision. The American pianist André Watts was his soloist on 20 May in Brahms's Second Concerto, and a November Russian programme in Dublin, Cork and Waterford had the Korean violinist Young-Uck Kim in Prokofiev's Second Concerto. Waterford was a notable addition to the regional circuit, after an absence of many years, and, due in large part to the dynamic music department at the Waterford Institute of Technology, is now an integral feature of the bi-annual NSO/*Irish Times* national tour.

1988 had also seen the First Dublin International Piano Competition in May. This now highly prestigious triennial event under the chairmanship of John O'Conor initially enjoyed the substantial sponsorship of the aircraft leasing firm, Guinness Peat Aviation and later of Guardian Insurance. The input of RTÉ has also become extensive with, among other things, the Orchestra being essential to the final two-day concerto rounds of the competition. The 1988 winner was the French artist Philippe Cassard, who has since pursued an international career but also retains a favoured place in the hearts of Dublin audiences.

The DGOS had a problematical Spring Season when difficulties arose with the Gaiety management. As a result the National Concert Hall became a theatre with a substantial set mounted on its platform and taking in the choir gallery behind it. The opera was Bellini's *Norma,* with Suzanne Murphy in the title role under the baton of Roderick Brydon. The production by Michael McCaffrey in a set designed by Ulderico Manani worked extremely well and had Angela Feeney as Adalgisa and Osvaldo di Pianduni as Pollione.

János Fürst

János Fürst began his musical career as a string player, studying at the Liszt Academy in his native Budapest, and later at the Paris Conservatoire, where he was a *premier prix*. While a member of the RÉSO, he founded the Irish Chamber Orchestra in 1963 and this marked the opening of his career as a conductor which saw him appointed as the RTÉSO's Principal in 1987/88. He has held similar positions in Malmö, Aalborg, Winterthur and at the opera in Marseilles, and was Chief Guest Conductor of the Helsinki Philharmonic. He became Head of Conducting Studies at the Paris Conservatoire in 1997.

9 November 1987
NCH

Frank Corcoran: Symphonies of Symphonies of Wind
Harty: The Children of Lir
Sibelius: Symphony no 2

Suzanne Murphy, soprano
János Fürst, conductor

13 November 1987
NCH

Brian Boydell: Symphonic Inscapes
Schubert: Symphony no 8
Richard Strauss: Don Quixote

Constantin Zanidache, viola
Ralph Kirschbaum, cello
János Fürst, conductor

27 May 1988
NCH

J C Bach: Symphony in D
Stravinsky: Symphony of Psalms
Prokofiev: Alexander Nevsky

Patricia Bardon, soprano
RTÉ Philharmonic Choir
Albert Rosen, conductor

3 June 1988
NCH

John Buckley: Symphony no 1*
Saint-Saëns: Piano Concerto no 2
Tchaikovsky: Francesca da Rimini

Veronica McSwiney, piano
Albert Rosen, conductor
**First performance*

A new kind of 'Proms'

In September 1989 new ground was broken when a series of 'Proms' was given in a specially erected marquee in the RTÉ grounds of Montrose. Sponsored by the tobacco company, Carroll's, and later by Bank of Ireland, these concerts proved to be an enormous success despite the far from satisfactory acoustics, and the fact that traffic noise from the nearby Stillorgan Road could not be properly stifled. But, with the Orchestra in less formal mood, the patrons were full of festive enthusiasm.

The 'Proms' created an audience and an atmosphere of their own which, despite a change of venue to the RDS Main Hall in Ballsbridge, continues unabated. In the first series the RTÉSO was conducted by Otmar Maga (with John O'Conor in Mozart's K 467 Concerto) and Colman Pearce. The then recent winner of the Cardiff Singer of the World Competition, Bryn Terfel, joined violinist Viktoria Mullova as Pearce's soloists.

After the carefree air of the 'Proms' Colman Pearce took the Orchestra through the rigours of 'Keqrops' by Iannis Xenakis, with the Australian pianist, Roger Woodward, who made a habit of indulging these difficult pieces. Two weeks later on 8 October Pearce dealt a blow for Shostakovich's Seventh, 'Leningrad', Symphony, after the Spanish pianist Joaquin Achucarro revived the least well known of Rachmaninov's Concertos, the Fourth.

In between, Albert Rosen conducted the first performance of John Kinsella's Second Symphony and renewed our acquaintance with Mahler's *Das Lied von der Erde* with Bernadette Greevy and John Mitchinson. Rosen was then part of the year's Wexford Festival when he conducted Marschner's *Der Templer und die Judin.* The Festival also included the first Irish performances of *The Duenna* which Prokofiev based on a Richard Brinsley Sheridan play.

As part of the celebrations for Dundalk's Heritage Year, the Orchestra revisited the town on 10 December after more than thirty years' absence. Colette McGahon, a native of the town, was heard in a number of Canteloube's 'Songs of the Auvergne', and as the alto in the solo quartet in Beethoven's Ninth Symphony with Virginia Kerr, Paul McCann, Andrew Murphy and Dundalk's Van Dessel Choir. The performance was previewed at the National Concert Hall two days earlier.

National Symphony Orchestra

1989/90 saw a further change in the precepts and practices of the Orchestra. Chief among these was the decision by the RTÉ Authority to redefine the Orchestra, and what since 1948 had been the RÉSO/RTÉSO became on 1 January 1990 the National Symphony Orchestra. In July 1989 the RTÉ Authority had decided to make a very substantial capital investment of £300,000 in its Symphony Orchestra's future. The band would be reconstituted and brought up to full international strength of ninety-three players. Steps were initiated to recruit an additional twenty-two musicians (the same number as the original 1948 Light Orchestra). The change would be 'the most significant departure in Irish orchestral activity since the RÉ Symphony was established in 1948'. One of the contributory factors to this decision had been an internal report by the Activity

8 July 1988
NCH

Beethoven: Symphony no 1
Beethoven: Symphony no 9

Virginia Kerr, soprano
Deirdre Cooling-Nolan, contralto
Peter Kerr, tenor
Frank O'Brien, bass
RTÉ Philharmonic Choir
Brian Wright, conductor

15 July 1988
NCH

Beethoven: Overture, Leonora no 2
Beethoven: Piano Concerto no 1
Beethoven: Symphony no 5

Peter Donohoe, piano
Lionel Friend, conductor

22 July 1988
NCH

Beethoven: Overture, Leonora no 1
Beethoven: Triple Concerto
Beethoven: Symphony no 7

Fionnuala Hunt, violin
Aisling Drury Byrne, cello
Una Hunt, piano
Colman Pearce, conductor

29 July 1988
NCH

Beethoven: Overture, Leonora no 3
Beethoven: Piano Concerto no 3
Beethoven: Symphony no 3 ('Eroica')

Jan Čap, piano
John Lubbock, conductor

17 June 1988
NCH

Haydn: Symphony no 83 ('La Poule')
Thea Musgrave: Clarinet Concerto
Tchaikovsky: Symphony no 4

Brian O'Rourke, clarinet
Peter Erös, conductor

5 July 1988
NCH (lunchtime)

Fleischmann: Times Offspring
Strauss: The Blue Danube
Mozart: Horn Concerto no 3, K447
Fauré: Dolly Suite

Lesley Bishop, horn
Eimear Ó Broin, conductor

6 January 1989
NCH

Mahler: Symphony no 3

Bernadette Greevy, contralto
Lindsay Singers
Palestrina Choir
János Fürst, conductor

13 January 1989
NCH

Wagner: Overture, 'Tannhäuser'
Dohnányi: Piano Concerto no 1
Mussorgsky/
Ravel: Pictures at an Exhibition

Helena Cesaro, piano
János Fürst, conductor

Review Unit, designed to make more cost-effective and dynamic use of resources available to RTÉ, bearing in mind its broadcasting and socio-cultural functions.

The position of General Manager was created and its first incumbent was Gareth Hudson, a practising musician and conductor who had had particular success with the Concert Orchestra and its 'Music For Fun' concerts which he had devised with Richard Pine. This post subsequently became 'Head of Orchestras and Performing Groups' giving the holder responsibility for both orchestras as well as the RTÉ String Quartet and the various choral ensembles.

Almost simultaneously John Kinsella was succeeded as Head of Music by Cathal McCabe who held the position until 1997. Frank Young had succeeded Val Keogh as Orchestra Manager, assisted by Patrick McElwee formerly of the Orchestra's horn section. Pat Dunleavy had succeeded Richard Pine as Concerts Manager and public relations were being handled by Laurie Cearr in the newly created post of Promotions Executive.

The new orchestral positions were advertised internationally and by means of this strategy it was hoped to attract home musicians who were then engaged with major orchestras overseas. There was some success with this strategy and, following trial periods, several artists from outside the country were employed . Nevertheless, to this day a number of the additional positions created in 1989 are held on a temporary or deputy basis.

George Hurst as Principal Conductor

The final and controversial element in this redefinition of the Symphony Orchestra was the decision, after some months' discussion, to appoint George Hurst as Principal Conductor. It was a surprise announcement, and sent shock waves through the Orchestra members. Hurst's previous encounter with them, in 1980, had been a difficult one. In addition to his then considerable involvement with the Bournemouth and BBC Scottish Orchestras, he had a substantial background as an orchestral trainer at the Guildhall School and the Dartington Summer School; he was a didactic figure not given to discussion, and temperamentally he and the Orchestra were not well suited.

The prospectus for the first season of the newly named orchestra had a 'Welcome from the General Manager' in which he stated that

> *'Above all, the evolution of the National Symphony Orchestra is a resounding confirmation of RTÉ's commitment to music in Ireland by making it possible to fulfil a more visible and accessible public function....the National Symphony Orchestra will not only undertake substantial series of subscription concerts but will also be involved right across the community in schools and universities, besides continuing the regular lunchtime events during the summer months'.*

It was felt in some quarters that this was little more than a restatement of the Orchestra's existing functions, although it was certainly intended to enhance those functions, not merely by means of a

George Hurst

Born in Edinburgh of Russian and Romanian parentage, George Hurst spent his early years in Canada, studying conducting with Pierre Monteux. He worked with the RPO before becoming Principal Conductor of the BBC Northern Symphony in 1958, later Principal Guest with the BBC Scottish Symphony, and subsequently holding positions with the Bournemouth Symphony and Sinfonietta. He also served as Consultant on Orchestral Studies with the National Centre for Orchestral Studies in London, besides directing many orchestral and conducting courses in Britain and elsewhere.

18 January 1989
NCH

Kodály: Peacock Variations
Bruch: Scottish Fantasy
Haydn: Mass in Time of War

Audrey Collins, violin
Kathleen Tynan, soprano
Deirdre Cooling-Nolan, contralto
Adrian Thompson, tenor
Nigel Williams, bass
RTÉ Philharmonic Choir
János Fürst, conductor
This concert was also performed in Cork on January 19th

27 January 1989
NCH

Haydn: Sinfonia Concertante
Bartók: Suite, 'Miraculous Mandarin'
Brahms: Symphony no 4

Matthew Manning, oboe
Michael Jones, bassoon
Fionnuala Hunt, violin
Aisling Drury Byrne, cello
János Fürst, conductor

26 May 1989
NCH

Mozart: Piano Concerto no 23 K488
Mahler: Symphony no 9

Aisling Heneghan, piano
János Fürst, conductor

change of name but also by creating new relationships with bodies outside RTÉ, not least the commercial and corporate sectors, and, above all, to facilitate a new artistic policy by revisiting the original objectives in the foundation of the Orchestra in the light of present day realities - not least of which was the need to expand the orchestra to international strength.

Thus, the same prospectus stated that it was RTÉ's intention to

> *'raise standards and to increase the status of the Orchestra with concert-goers both in its home base at the National Concert Hall and also throughout Ireland - in particular for the younger listeners who will form the National Symphony Orchestra's audience of the future'.*

The most immediate effect of this aspiration was to offer the paying public a number of booking choices which came on stream through a flexible system of arrangements for all or part of the season's concerts, and this has been an increasingly visible factor in the marketing strategy for NCH concerts since that time.

The NSO's opening gambit was on 5 January 1990 with Hurst conducting and the programme had the solid basis of Schumann's Piano Concerto with Hugh Tinney and the Brahms First Symphony. The composer's Second and Third Symphonies and Violin Concerto would also figure during the year but the Russian side of the Principal Conductor's ancestry showed on 17 January through Stravinsky's Firebird and Tchaikovsky's Violin Concerto with Dong-Suk Kang.

There were other spectacular events during the year with the return of the Messiaen entourage for another performance of his *Turangalîla-symphonie*, again through the support of the Cultural Services of the French Embassy. John Carewe conducted this time and the excitement and enthusiasm of the audience was no less lavish than in the SFX Hall some fourteen years previously. Messiaen's reception was rapturous.

On another contemporary front Thérèse Timoney, who had been a member of the RTÉSO and leader of the Cologne Chamber Orchestra, gave the first performance of her husband John Kinsella's Second Violin Concerto on 9 March with Albert Rosen. EJ Moeran's Cello Concerto resurfaced on 14 March through Raphael Wallfisch and Proinnsías Ó Duinn, while Eric Sweeney's cantata 'Deirdre' (an RTÉ commission) had its premiere under Colman Pearce on 6 April. The soloists in this Ulick O'Connor setting were Kathleen Tynan and Peter McBrien with the RTÉ Chamber Choir and Sweeney's own Waterford College Choir.

The NSO gathered in the Gaiety pit for the DGOS Spring season and the first Irish production of Britten's *Peter Grimes*. Conducted by Simon Joly, the title role and that of Ellen Orford were sung by the American artists William Neill and Pamela Myers. Artistically successful, it was a financial disaster and went some way to forcing the abandonment of the Society's 1990 Winter Season at the Gaiety.

2 June 1989
NCH

Verdi: Requiem

Suzanne Murphy, soprano
Liljana Nejceva, contralto
Lawrence Bakst, tenor
Wout Oosterkamp, bass
RTÉ Philharmonic Choir
János Fürst, conductor

28 July 1989
NCH

Mozart: Symphony no 35, K385
Mozart: Ch'io mi scordi di te, K505
Tchaikovsky: Symphony no 6 ('Pathétique')

Marie Walshe, mezzo-soprano
János Fürst, conductor
This was János Fürst's final concert as Principal Conductor

25 February 1989
NCH

Verdi: Overture, 'Sicilian Vespers'
Beethoven: Piano Concerto no 3
Stravinsky: The Rite of Spring

Chantal Bohets, piano
Kasper de Roo, conductor

30 June 1989
NCH

Brian Boydell: Masai Mara*
Mozart: Piano Concerto no 15, K450
Bruckner: Symphony no 4

Courtney Kenny, piano
Kasper de Roo, conductor
**First performance*

23 February 1990
NCH

Beethoven: Missa Solemnis

Julie Kennard, soprano
Bernadette Greevy, contralto
Andrew Murgatroyd, tenor
Nigel Williams, bass
RTÉ Philharmonic Choir
George Hurst, conductor

1 March 1990
NCH

Glinka: Overture, 'Ruslan and Ludmilla'
Rachmaninov: Piano Concerto no 3
Berlioz: Symphonie fantastique

Mícheál O'Rourke, piano
George Hurst, conductor
This concert was performed in Belfast on 2 March

18 May 1990
NCH

James Wilson: Angel Two*
Rachmaninov: Piano Concerto no 2
Tchaikovsky: Symphony no 2

Howard Shelley, piano
George Hurst, conductor
**First performance*

Celebrity concerts

Another aspect of the NSO's new life was a series of engagements with major entertainment figures, several of them from the world of international opera, which also saw the Orchestra appearing at unusual venues. The first of these took place at Simmonscourt, part of the RDS complex at Ballsbridge, and better known for livestock sales, circus tents, ice rinks and carnival activities, which took on the role of Concert Hall on 4 April when the Orchestra moved there to accompany Luciano Pavarotti. It was a far cry from his first Dublin appearances with the DGOS in 1963 and 1964 and prices were in a different category as well. But this was the first of a number of extravaganzas in which the Orchestra would shine superbly in the company of superstars such as Placido Domingo, Kiri te Kanawa, José Carreras, Monserrat Caballé (accompanied in part by Finbar Wright) and, in 1991, Pavarotti again - these taking place at the Point Theatre, a former bonded warehouse built in 1878 for the ocean-going trade, converted into a multi-purpose, large capacity entertainment house where RTÉ has been involved in many spectacular show business events, including three presentations of the Eurovision Song Contest featuring the Concert Orchestra.

In July, the musicians travelled to Co Limerick for the first Adare Festival where a number of performances took place in a specially erected marquee. It was similar to the 'Proms' tent in Montrose but because of the pastoral setting noise intrusion was virtually nil. The programme, with cellist Julian Lloyd Webber as soloist in Saint-Saëns, was mainly French, although conductor Colin Metters chose the Sibelius First as his Symphony.

Following the annual Wexford engagement the NSO paid a unique tribute to Uachtarán na hÉireann, Dr Patrick Hillery, on 16 November, just a short while before he retired from office. Aptly called 'Omós don Uachtarán', Proinnsías Ó Duinn conducted two of Dr Hillery's favourite pieces, the Mozart Clarinet Concerto (John Finucane) and Beethoven's Fifth Symphony. Gerard Victory produced a commissioned ceremonial piece, also entitled 'Omós don Uachtarán', to set the concert in train. It was another one of those glittering 'nights to remember'.

Resignation of George Hurst

A Broadcasting Bill introduced into the Oireachtas by the Minister for Communications, Ray Burke, TD, was sending ominous signals through the corridors of power in RTÉ. Part of this would impose a restriction on advertising revenue to RTÉ, which in turn would dictate belt-tightening measures throughout the organisation. In the Music Department the planned increases in the permanent strength of the Orchestra might not be possible. A number of positions in the NSO's rank and file, announced with great delight in 1989, had been filled on a temporary basis during the past year but it now looked as if those currently employed in this way might not be established. The musicians were distressed at the possibility that the plans for the NSO might be abandoned. In addition, they were unable to accept a provision for NSO concerts to be augmented by members of the RTÉCO,

National Concert Hall

26 September 1990
NCH

Martinů: Symphony no 6*
Schumann: Cello Concerto
Dvořák: Slavonic Dances op 46

Steven Isserlis, cello
George Hurst, conductor
This concert was repeated in Cork on 27 September

5 October 1990
NCH

Dvořák: Scherzo Capriccioso
Martinů: Symphony no 4*
Brahms: Violin Concerto

Gyorgy Pauk, violin
George Hurst, conductor

**commemorating the Martinů centenary*

and took industrial action, with the result that a number of concerts were lost. In the wake of this action George Hurst, whose position as a musician with management responsibilities had become invidious, resigned. His resignation was accepted but he was asked to abide by that part of his contract which necessitated him to tour with the NCH to Germany in 1992 and this he agreed to do. The affair however meant a number of replacement conductors would be needed for 1991 and the gaps were filled by Albert Rosen, Jacek Kaspszyk, Hubert Soudant, Proinnsías Ó Duinn and Colman Pearce.

RTÉ decided to invite Bryden Thomson to return as Principal Conductor. Despite knowing that he was dying of cancer, he accepted the appointment. Since his marriage to the pianist and teacher Mary Ellison, his home was in Dublin. Alas, the appointment was not to be. Bryden Thomson (or Jack, as he was affectionately known in the business) died in November. The shock was palpable as the disease had already taken principal viola Archie Collins, husband of Audrey Park, in 1988, and double-bass player, Herbert Nowak in 1990. Sadly history would repeat itself within a relatively short time.

At the beginning of 1991 Audrey Collins (she was now using her marriage name) was leading, with Clodagh Vedres acting as co-leader. The first violins also included Camilla Gunzl, Claire Crehan, Patrick Fitzgerald Mooney, Audrey McAllister, Cong Gu, Ting-Zhong Deng and Brona Fitzgerald. Keith Packer, Mary Wheatley, Briege McGoldrick and Fiona McAuslan were in the seconds, and Séamus O'Grady was now leading the violas. Neil Martin, Randal Devine and Helena Plews were also there, while Lindsay Martindale, Rosemary Elliott, Lyssa Fergus and Annette Cleary formed part of the cello line. Séamus Doyle, Waldemar Kozak, Daniel Whibley and Joszef Csibi, Junior, were now in the double-basses.

William Dowdall was leading flute, with Deirdre Brady alternating third flute and piccolo. Ruby Ashley was second oboe; Paul Roe and Fintan Sutton were in the clarinets; Ian Dakin and David Atcheler in the horns; Graham Hastings in the trumpets. Noel Eccles was leading percussion, assisted by Angela Dakin, Paul Maher and Stephen Keogh, with Lynda Byrne doubling piano and celeste. Gareth Hudson was listed as General Manager and Patrick McElwee had become Orchestra Manager. Pat Dunleavy was now Concerts Manager with Maureen Donohoe Planning Coordinator and Bene McAteer the Librarian. The Orchestral Assistants were Séamus McDonnell, Liam Hennessy and Daniel McDonnell.

Commercial recordings

Prior to its commercial recording with the NSO and RTÉ Philharmonic on the Argo label, Balfe's opera *The Bohemian Girl* had a performance at the NCH on 13 January 1991 under the baton of the distinguished Richard Bonynge. The title role was sung by Nova Thomas, a protegée of Joan Sutherland, Bonynge's wife, who came to Dublin for the occasion. It was the beginning of a new era in the Orchestra's history. Up to this point the Orchestra's discography was extremely limited - only a very few token

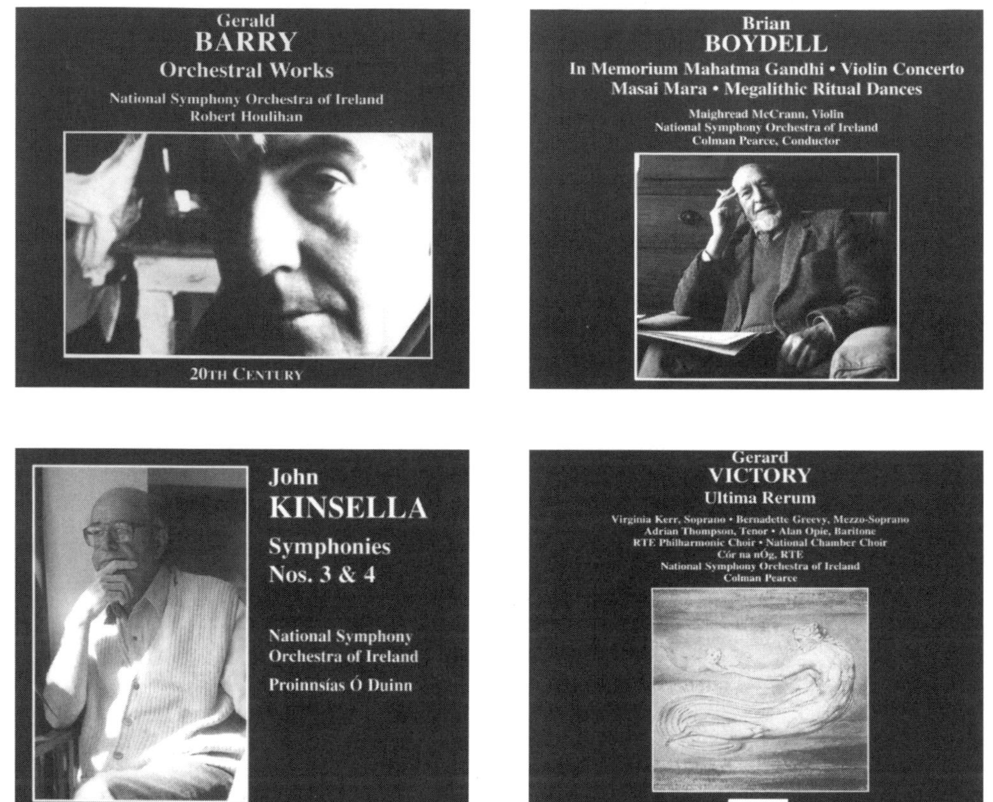
Gerald
BARRY
Orchestral Works
National Symphony Orchestra of Ireland
Robert Houlihan
20TH CENTURY
Brian
BOYDELL
In Memorium Mahatma Gandhi • Violin Concerto
Masai Mara • Megalithic Ritual Dances
Maighread McCrann, Violin
National Symphony Orchestra of Ireland
Colman Pearce, Conductor
John
KINSELLA
Symphonies
Nos. 3 & 4
National Symphony
Orchestra of Ireland
Proinnsías Ó Duinn
Gerard
VICTORY
Ultima Rerum
Virginia Kerr, Soprano • Bernadette Greevy, Mezzo-Soprano
Adrian Thompson, Tenor • Alan Opie, Baritone
RTE Philharmonic Choir • National Chamber Choir
Cór na nÓg, RTE
National Symphony Orchestra of Ireland
Colman Pearce
2CD's

recordings had been made: very early discs included two selections of Irish music recorded under Horvat in the late 1950s for the US market, and another, entitled 'Ireland, Mother Ireland,' with the Orchestra accompanying Our Lady's Choral Society, was issued in 1964. Bernadette Greevy and Harold Gray were the soloists and JM Doyle conducted the selection of Irish music which marked the first time a commercial company, in fact Argo, recorded Irish music with such a large choir and orchestra. A limited vinyl release of Seoirse Bodley's 'Ceol', live from the opening of the National Concert Hall and coupled with AJ Potter's 'Sinfonia De Profundis', was issued in 1981, and otherwise a recording in 1973 of Boydell's 'Symphonic Inscapes', coupled with Victory's 'Jonathan Swift' on the NIRC label was its only major publication.

But in 1992 RTÉ signed a substantial contract with the Naxos/Marco Polo company and quite soon the NSO had launched into a series of sessions which began in June 1992, with Adrian Leaper directing two of the Symphonies (Nos 17 and 32) of that enigmatic figure Havergal Brian for Marco Polo. The same label also issued the first of a substantial number of CDs devoted to Irish composers. Pride of place fell to the double album of Gerard Victory's *Ultima Rerum* which was recorded under Colman Pearce in December 1992.

Stanford's *Requiem* was the next Irish issue, while a CD of works by Brian Boydell, again with Colman Pearce, and Maighréad McCrann in the Violin Concerto, was recorded in January 1995. Music by Philip Martin, including his Harp Concerto with Andreja Malíř, was also recorded in January. Some of John Buckley's output, including his Organ Concerto with Peter Sweeney, went on disc in May 1995 together with John Kinsella's Third and Fourth Symphonies under Proinnsías Ó Duinn, recorded in January 1996.

Works by James Wilson (mainly his Viola and Violin Concertos, with Constantin Zanidache and Alan Smale) followed in April that year, while a selection of Gerald Barry was in the can by the end of May 1996. Raymond Deane's Oboe Concerto, 'Krespel's Concerto' (violin), and 'Quaternion' for piano and orchestra were recorded in June 1997. Colman Pearce was again conducting with (respectively) soloists Matthew Manning, Alan Smale and Anthony Byrne.

The unusual nature of the Wexford Festival's repertoire brought live recordings of Rubinstein's *The Demon* from 1994 (Alexander Anissimov), Pacini's *Saffo* of 1995 (Maurizio Benini) and Meyerbeer's *L'Etoile du Nord* from the 1996 Festival (Wladimir Jurowski).

On the Naxos side, Adrian Leaper has conducted the Nielsen Symphonies and Stefan Sanderling the Tchaikovsky Suites. Gerhard Markson is currently involved with Mendelssohn, and Alexander Anissimov is going through the Rachmaninov Symphonies, *The Bells,* and a number of the smaller orchestral works. Mahler's *Das Lied von der Erde* with Ruxandra Donose and Thomas Harper under Michael Halasz, and his *Lieder eines fahrenden Gesellen, Kindertotenlieder* and 'Rückert' Lieder have come from Bernadette Greevy with János Fürst and Franz Paul Decker.

programme
23rd - 30th May 1992
Bank of Ireland RTE
Proms

In May 1994 Maria Kliegel recorded the Schumann Cello Concerto and the Brahms Double Concerto with Ilya Kaler. The conductor was Andrew Constantine, and in May 1995 Maria Kliegel undertook Bloch's 'Schelomo' and Tchaikovsky's Rococo Variations under Gerhard Markson. Following the famous Point performances, Verdi's *Aida* went on a double album in October 1994. The conductor then was Rico Saccani and he returned to record music by Respighi in September 1995.

The Carrolls 'Proms' in 1991 had Orff's *Carmina Burana* on 21 May and a Tchaikovsky evening which included the Army No 1 Band for the '1812' Overture and Stoika Milanova in the Violin Concerto on 25 May. Bryden Thomson conducted and entered into the spirit of the occasion with unbridled enthusiasm. He had musicians and audience eating out of his hand. In July the Orchestra returned to Adare where it gave an 'Irish Classics' evening on 21st (Ó Riada's 'Mise Éire'; John Field Second Piano Concerto with Mícéál O'Rourke and Shaun Davey's 'The Relief of Derry' Symphony) with Gearóid Grant conducting.

New Irish Music

New Irish music during 1991 included the premieres of Fergus Johnston's 'Samsara' (Colman Pearce on 14 June) which like Philip Martin's Second Piano Concerto on 21 June was an RTÉ commission, although the Concerto also had the backing of the Dublin European City of Culture 1991 Committee. Martin subtitled his piece 'A Day in the City' and dedicated it to his first teacher, Mabel Swainson.

Gerald Barry's *'Chevaux de frise'*, written for the 400th anniversary of the Spanish Armada, had its first NSO performance on 28 June when Robert Houlihan, who had directed the London premiere in 1988, conducted. Colman Pearce took charge of Gerard Victory's Fourth Symphony on 12 July in a concert where Peter Donohoe played the Brahms Second Piano Concerto.

The second Accents Festival, (the first Festival had not employed the Orchestra directly, although Eric Sweeney's 'Deirdre' was premiered during it) devised by the Association of Irish Composers, also focused on contemporary music, and the NSO's concert at the RHA Gallery on 10 September repeated Raymond Deane's 'Thresholds', but with Colman Pearce conducting this time. The remainder of the programme was devoted to premieres of RTÉ commissions - John Kinsella's Third Symphony and Walter Beckett's 'Dublin' Symphony, which had Anna Manahan reciting Rhoda Coghill's poem 'In the City' in the Prologue, and an extract from Joyce's *Finnegans Wake* in the Epilogue.

It is often remarked by its critics that RTÉ neglects, or fails to adequately promote, the work of contemporary composers. But the record which has been adduced here, of both Irish and international works by a wide range of twentieth century composers, should set that record straight. In an age of financial stringency, programmes must of necessity be tailored towards popular taste, but, box-office demands notwithstanding, the NSO has presented a substantial body of modern work and, in its current 'Music Now!' policy, is regularly commissioning new

Kasper de Roo

music in association with the two Arts Councils in Ireland and the Ulster Orchestra.

There was a certain air of novelty on 20 September 1991 when Donal Bannister, a former RTÉ 'Musician of the Future', was heard in Launy Grondahl's Trombone Concerto and earlier in the year (May) the Second GPA Dublin International Piano Competition had the Orchestra again involved in its final rounds. The winner was the brilliant young Russian, Pavel Nersessian. This again is a symptom of RTÉ's willingness to engage with, and support, new musical initiatives where they offer an extra dimension to Irish cultural life and where the resources of the NSO are the most appropriate and available to be committed to their fulfilment.

A further dimension to the National Concert Hall came on 28 September 1991 also, when the Orchestra was part of the grand inauguration of its Philip Jones Organ. The magnificent instrument had taken some time to build and indeed caused occasional inconvenience to the musicians as well as demanding the Hall's closure for two brief periods. Peter Hurford and Gerard Gillen did the opening honours with Professor Gillen the soloist in the Saint-Saëns Third (Organ) Symphony. Proinnsías Ó Duinn conducted on another glittering occasion.

Appointment of Kasper de Roo

The New Year 1992 was not without its problems for management. There was still a Principal Conductor to be appointed, and a replacement for the concerts already allocated to Bryden Thomson had to be found. A new system was introduced at this point which saw the Orchestra personnel having a direct input into the selection process for Principal Conductors. Henceforth a Principal could be not appointed who was unacceptable to both the Orchestra and the RTÉ management, and on this basis Kees Bakels, who had made a very favourable impression with the Orchestra and the public in his previous appearances, was offered the vacant position.

Unfortunately, this method of selection was not entirely without its pitfalls, since Mr Bakels began to require changes in orchestral personnel which neither the players nor the management could countenance. However necessary it was - and is - to reposition players at various stages in their professional lives, it was bad practice to do so in a peremptory fashion and without consultation. In the end, differences with Kees Bakels could not be resolved and he was unable to take up his appointment.

Because eligible musicians already have contractual arrangements in place, the lead time for an appointment of such importance is likely to be one of at least several months if not a couple of years, and in this instance, although another firm favourite emerged from discussion with the Orchestra, it would be the end of 1993 before Kasper de Roo was announced as the eventual successor to George Hurst, and February 1994 before he undertook his inaugural concert.

Part of Bakels's contract had included the commitment to record the Nielsen symphonies for Naxos, and in due course he was replaced in this project by Adrian

1992 German Press Comments

From the Wolfsburger *Allgemeine Zeitung* on the Brahms Variations

"The interpretation of the Dublin Orchestra, outstanding in all its sections, reached, in breath and magnitude of the form, a level that reminded one of performances under Furtwängler.... Prolonged applause, indeed ovations, rewarded the guests from Ireland for a concert-evening that will long remain in the memory".

From the *Kieler Nachrichten* on Shostakovich

"Hurst....led his musicians in a structurally transparent performance of the complicated symphonic process. The intensity of the expression emanated from the extremely distinctive sounds of the individual instruments".

From the *Wilhelmshavener Zeitung* on the Brahms Symphony

"The woodwind section played with the finest intonation, the brass achieved an admirable precision in embouchure and the strings excelled with sometimes forcefully attacked, sometimes tenderly sung, melodies".

From the *Emder Zeitung* on the Hindemith and Brahms Symphony

"This was a dazzling start with timpani and trumpets. Sometimes fierce, (but never unbearable), using all wind and percussion instruments, sometimes tender, with almost inaudible strings, the orchestra under George Hurst made this piece the real event of the evening....They enthralled the audience with very sophisticated and precise playing".

And from a Witten paper on the Spohr soloists

"Christoph Poppen, the violinist, coloured his interpretation with a stressed, soft and dark sound quality. In the harpist, Ursula Holliger, the Professor of Music from Detmold found a superlative partner who complemented the violin with a vigorous and exciting interpretation".

From the magazine *Kultur* on the Hindemith and Sweeney

"The Irish guests, playing with great discipline, also gave an impressive account of the closing March....It was as if glumly stamping Hindemith ostinatos, very slightly changed, had lost their way in the channels of repetitive "minimal music" when the Irish presented "Dance Music" by their fellow countryman Eric Sweeney. It was quite entertaining, "dissonance free" music with a dominant clear sound and a memorable (also five-part) rhythmic pattern.... The likeable guests said good-bye with a Schubert encore".

And finally from Jurgen Schmidt on the same concert

"The Second Symphony of Brahms.....which conjured up a summer idyll in the first movement, was....the crowning event of the evening. The Irish seem to have a particularly sensitive understanding of the deep emotions of the North German composer. Bravissimo!"

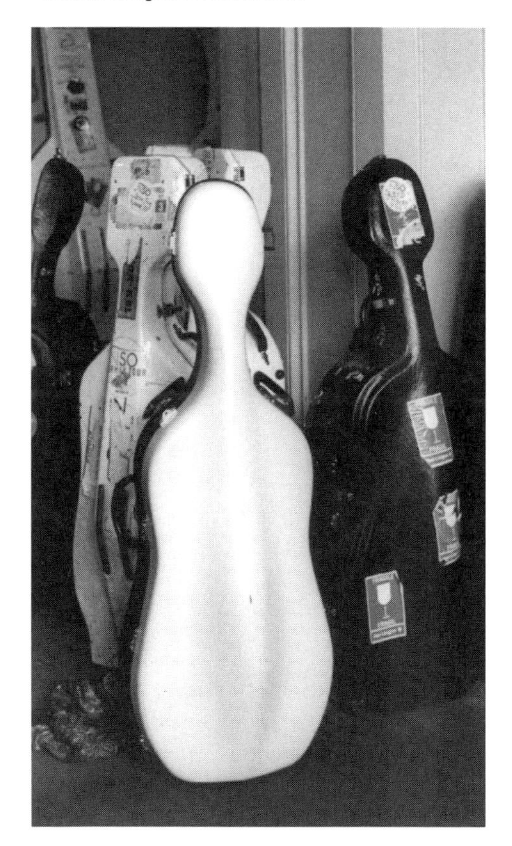

Leaper, who completed the cycle to great acclaim in 1995

In the meantime, the Orchestra went to The Point again to take part in the 400th anniversary celebrations of Dublin's Trinity College. The venue was demanded by the space required for Mahler's gigantic Eighth Symphony. There were two performances on 14 and 15 April 1992, conducted by the Welsh artist Owain Arwel Hughes. For it the NSO forces were joined to RTÉ's Concert Orchestra and the assembly of choirs for this 'Symphony of a Thousand' drawn from Cantique, Culwick, Dún Laoghaire, Goethe Institute, Guinness, Musica Sacra, Our Lady's, RTÉ's Philharmonic and Cór na nÓg and Dublin University itself. The soloists were sopranos Jo-Ann Pickens, Julie Kennard and Mary Hegarty; altos Bernadette Greevy and Catherine Denley; tenor John Mitchinson; baritone Jason Howard; and bass David Wilson-Johnson. The celebratory 'Flamboys' by Gerald Barry acted as a brief 'curtain-raiser'.

The NSO returned to Adare in July for two concerts under Marco Guidarini and Albert Rosen. Joaquin Achucarro played Chopin's Second Concerto at the first, and Dmitri Alexeev Mozart's D minor K 466 in the second. Maestro Guidarini repeated Amcrican/Irish Jane O'Leary's first orchestral work, 'Islands of Discovery', in Adare, having introduced the piece at the NCH on 17 July.

New music during the year also included the premiere of John Kinsella's Fourth Symphony (Proinnsías Ó Duinn), the first performance in the Republic of Schnittke's Cello Concerto (Torlief Thedeen and Matthias Bamert), and another revival of Gerard Victory's *Ultima Rerum* (Colman Pearce).

Tour of Germany

By far the most exciting event of 1992 for the Orchestra was its extensive autumn tour to Germany under George Hurst, managed by Simon Taylor, who had succeeded Gareth Hudson as Head of Orchestras and Performing Groups. The programmes were previewed at the National Concert Hall on 11 and 18 September and the tour, sponsored by Aer Lingus, commenced on the 21st and continued until 4 October, taking in visits to Wolfsburg, Kiel, Wilhelmshaven, Emden, Witten, Erlangen, Stuttgart, Ingolstadt, Leverkusen and Bielefeld.

The programmes included Eric Sweeney's 'Dance Music', Hindemith's 'Weber Metamorphoses', the curio of Spohr's Concertante No 2 for Violin and Harp with Christoph Poppen and Ursula Holliger, Brahms's 'St Anthony' Variations and Second Symphony, and Shostakovich's Tenth Symphony. The Stuttgart concert was retransmitted directly to RTÉ from Suddeutscher Rundfunk.

The Orchestra was extremely well received throughout the tour.

Not so exhilarating was a short visit to Leeds, Liverpool and Belfast the next year (1993). Although artistically successful, audiences were poor and the euphoria of the earlier tours was not repeated this time round.

The orchestral line-up in June 1993 had Michael D'Arcy as deputy leader (he

Miċeál O'Rourke and Albert Rosen in rehearsal, 1982

John O'Conor

would be appointed leader of the Concert Orchestra in time), and the violins included Catherine Briscoe and Anna Kane, David Clark and Ann Harte, Sheila O'Grady and Ruth Murphy. Cornelia Sexton, Rosalind Brown and Louis Roden were in the second violins; and Cheremie Allum, John Kelly and Vivienne Atcheler among the viola ranks. William Butt, Una Ní Chanainn and Arum Roa were found in the cellos. Caitríona Ryan was doubling flute and piccolo and Killyan Bannister and Mark O'Keeffe had joined the trumpet line. Szabolcs Vedres was Management Assistant and Donal O'Sullivan had become an Orchestral Assistant.

In September 1993 the NSO had the pleasant duty of travelling to Limerick for the official opening of its University Concert Hall on 18th. As had been the case at the NCH in 1981, Colman Pearce was on the rostrum. There was a commissioned work from John Buckley, a native of nearby Templeglantine in 1951, who decided on a piece for speakers and large orchestra, 'Rivers of Paradise', with suitable academic texts by John Donne, Marlowe, Shakespeare, Johann Kepler, John Henry Newman and TS Eliot. Barry Douglas played Beethoven's Fifth Concerto and the symphony was Dvořák's 'New World'.

There was an ample supply of new works during 1994, starting with Lutoslawski's Piano Concerto from Mícéal O'Rourke and Russian conductor Vladimir Altschüler in Dublin and Belfast on 2 and 3 February. John Kinsella's Fifth Symphony, subtitled '1916 Poets' - material from Joseph Mary Plunkett, Thomas MacDonagh and Pádraig Pearse - had its premiere through Colman Pearce on 18 February. Four days later Mr Pearce introduced Seoirse Bodley's Fourth Symphony to Ireland, its premiere having taken place in Parma in July 1991.

John Buckley's 'Rivers of Paradise' had an NCH performance also on 18 February, and James Wilson's Viola Concerto, 'Menorah', its first public performance four days later. Wilson's orchestral Concertino, an RTÉ commission and with a flexaphone in the percussion, was given its premiere by Colman Pearce on 15 April. Robert Lamb conducted his own 'Children of Lir' for the first time on 1 July with the actress Fiona Shaw.

The then popular Third Symphony of Henryk Gorecki, the 'Symphony of Sorrowful Songs', had its first Irish performance under Jerzy Maksymiuk and Agnieszka Kurowska, soprano, on 18 November, when Peter Frankl played Schnittke's Piano Concerto in Ireland for the first time as well. Celebrating his ninetieth birthday a little early Michael Tippett travelled from his home in England to attend a special concert of his own music at the NCH on 9 December 1994. Colman Pearce conducted the Fourth Symphony and the Yeats-inspired 'Byzantium' with Virginia Kerr. The composer declared himself immensely satisfied with the performances.

PIANO review group

During 1994 the Minister for Arts, Culture and the Gaeltacht, Mr Michael D Higgins, TD, set up a review group - Provision and Institutional Arrangements Now for Orchestras and Ensembles (PIANO) to examine, among other things:

> *'the roles as they have evolved of the performing groups in RTÉ with particular reference to which the broadcasting and non-broadcasting demands are compatible and to make whatever recommendations it considers desirable regarding the organisational arrangements that would enhance the development of the groups'.*

The review was considered necessary because it was recognised that, as the Report stated, 'from humble beginnings' the music groups associated with broadcasting had grown in size and importance, and RTÉ's role as a major employer of musicians, a major provider of music programming and source of commissions for new music, required some examination. This was particularly so in the potential incompatibility of broadcasting and non-broadcasting functions.

PIANO was chaired by Dr John O'Conor and the group comprised John Horgan, Loretta Keating, John Kinsella and Dr Geraldine O'Grady and they would deliberate for almost two years before issuing their report.

The PIANO committee reported in January 1996. In a substantial document considerable space was given to the structure and management of the NSO. It was suggested that the Orchestra should in fact move out from under the immediate control of RTÉ and be linked to the Department of the Minister for the Arts, Culture and the Gaeltacht. It should be governed by a sixteen-member Board which would be appointed by the Minister.The NSO should be funded initially by RTÉ's income from the licence fee, and, in the long-term, its running costs would come from central funds. The Orchestra should be set up as a Company Limited by Guarantee. Priority should be given to strengthening the Orchestra sections by creating more named posts. This would help spread the workload of these very demanding positions which require much preparatory work in advance of the first rehearsal for each concert.

The report also gave an interesting table of accounts which showed the Orchestra's funding in 1994 to be £3.7 million, of which only £580,000 came from concert income. The Report also made the point that legislation would be needed to underpin its security as an institution, and that security of funding and employment were essential. The public profile of the NSO should also be enhanced and modern marketing strategies employed in advancing this procedure. PIANO also recommended that members of the new Board be appointed in the Spring of 1996, that a Chief Executive be in place by the end of the year, and that the new structures should take effect from 1 September 1997.

At the end of 1997, no action has been taken on these recommendations, but in recognition of the proposals RTÉ itself has moved to embrace the broad thrust of the proposals by announcing its intention to relocate not only the NSO but all its music groups within a new structure which will protect their integrity and facilitate a more effective promotion of managerial and artistic strategies. This represents a major shift of focus for the NSO in particular, as it has up to now been located within the Radio Division and funded therefrom. The establishment

Audrey Park

Scottish-born Audrey Park lived in Ireland from 1952. She studied with Jaroslav Vaneček and first joined the RTÉSO in 1953. From 1966 to 1971 she was a member of the RTÉ String Quartet, before becoming Leader of the RTÉ Concert Orchestra and, in 1979, of the RTÉ Symphony. She was also an outstanding chamber music player, in latter years leading the Testore Quartet, named after her own instrument, made in 1710 in Milan by Giuseppe Testore.

of a separate Division within RTÉ, with a new post of Director of Music (advertised in late 1997) reporting directly to the Director-General, is a timely redefinition of the premier Irish orchestra in terms of both broadcasting and public performance functions.

The loss of colleagues

On Sunday 26 March 1995 members of the NSO, RTÉ Concert Orchestra and some free-lance musicians gave a special 'Daffodil Day' concert at the NCH to celebrate the life of Audrey Park Collins who had died in December 1994. In so doing they also remembered a number of other deceased RTÉ musicians who had suffered from cancer, among them Audrey's husband, Archie (1988), the colourful and aristocratic Spanish violinist Carlos Assa-Munt (1992) and the outstanding young horn player Ray Cavanagh (1993).

The concert also commemorated the charming and dedicated French violinist Jack Leydier (1994); the self-effacing Charles Maguire (1993), one of the famous family of musicians who served in both RTÉ Orchestras; the highly accomplished German double-bass player, Herbert Nowak (1990); Bryden Thomson (1991), internationally renowned and highly admired here; and the extraordinary Gerard Victory, who had died just a few weeks earlier.

The programme book contained several tributes to Audrey Park. There was one from Uachtarán na hÉireann, Mary Robinson, and another from Kasper de Roo, but I quote from Alan Smale, who became the NSO's leader in 1994:

> *'I worked closely with Audrey for many years, including four as her co-leader. Although contrasting in style and temperament, we had great affection and respect for each other as ultimately our beliefs and musical aims were the same. When I left the Symphony to lead the Concert Orchestra in 1984 Audrey offered me no advice - that was not her style....but as the years went by I understood at first hand the joys, difficulties and sacrifices that go hand in hand with a leader's position and the single mindedness that cannot be shared even with very close colleagues...We are here today and every day, to experience the healing energy of music and to share that with each other and with audiences everywhere. Audrey understood this deeply and it is the best way I can think of to remember her'.*

The concert was conducted in the main by Vladimir Altschüler but Fergus O'Carroll, one of the horn players who has developed a freelance conducting career, took the opening Copland 'Fanfare for the Common Man'. John O'Conor was the soloist in Beethoven's Third Concerto and Bill Whelan contributed an affectionate memorial in his 'Pictures of Audrey'. The first part of the evening, entitled 'A Daffodil Day Concert', was recorded on compact disc in aid of the Irish Cancer Society. It remains a happy reminder of some wonderful people.

Similarly, Colman Pearce also contributed a worthy obituary for Gerard Victory in the NSO's programme book for the *Irish Times* national tour in March. Conducted by Vladimir Altschüler, the concerts in

Alan Smale

Season in Hong Kong

The young Shanghai conductor Long Yu conducted a Chinese programme on 5 and 6 August, when Japanese Takako Nishizaki was the soloist in the Butterfly Lovers' Violin Concerto - a work from the combined efforts of He Zhanhao and Chen Gang. There was a concert "From the Silver Screen" (Mozart's Symphony No 29, used in Amadeus; and Wagner's Ride of the Valkyries, from Apocalypse Now) on 7th again with Mr Yu.

The other three events were conducted by Gerhard Markson, beginning with "Classics for Leisure", when Rodrigo's Concierto de Aranjuez (Norbert Kraft) and Tchaikovsky's Pathétique Symphony were the main items. Harty's A Fair Day also had an oriental outing here.

"A Seat at the Opera" the following evening covered music by Mozart, Rossini, Verdi and Puccini, and had the singers Angelina Ruzzafante, Marilyn Bennett, Arturo Valencia and Markus Brueck in solo arias and ensembles. The final concert, "Dancing on the Green", on 11 August included Ravel's La Valse, Falla's Three Cornered Hat and the Polovtsian Dances from Borodin's

Dublin, Galway, Limerick, Cork and Waterford opened with the Aubade from Victory's delightful 'From Renoir's Workshop', which in fact Albert Rosen had premiered in 1974. Pearce's obituary tribute to Dr Victory read in part:

> *'His Directorship was remarkable for his broad vision, catholicity of musical taste, for his fostering of native talent, both performing and compositional. He was scrupulously fair and these were bountiful years for Irish composers. On a personal note, Gerry was a stalwart champion of my career, and I owe so much to his belief in my talents, and to his unswerving loyalty. But many Irish artists have cause to feel grateful for his unselfish and enlightened advocacy......He was one of the very few people I've known that I would unhesitatingly call a genius'.*

On a happier note, the NSO joined Our Lady's Choral Society for its fiftieth birthday celebrations in February 1995. Proinnsías Ó Duinn, the choir's Music Director, conducted Elgar's *The Kingdom* on 11th and *The Apostles* the following evening. It was an unique opportunity of hearing the two works back to back and an occasion unlikely to be repeated for some time. The birthday soloists were Lynda Lee, Bernadette Greevy, Paul Charles Clarke, Frank O'Brien, Michael Pearce and Ian Caddy.

The opening concert of 1996, on New Year's Day, was an RTÉ Gala, celebrating 'Seventy Years of Irish Broadcasting'. The NSO was under the baton of Albert Rosen with solo soprano, Mary Hegarty and tenor, Patrick Power. It was a light hearted-affair and included a commissioned 'Festival Overture' from John Kinsella. This, like Boydell's 'Jubilee Music' a decade earlier, featured the tune 'O'Donnell Abú' and started with Kevin Roche's arrangement for harp and celeste which was broadcast as the Station's call-sign from the mid-1950s onwards and was very familiar to all radio listeners.

A tour to the orient

The NSO broke new ground during 1996 by taking its first tour outside Europe. As a result of the connection with Naxos, the Orchestra was invited to give six concerts in seven days in Hong Kong during August. It was a hectic schedule but one which seemed to identify with the hustle and bustle of the location.

All the concerts took place in the magnificent new Hong Kong Culture Centre Concert Hall, with an acoustic which allowed the NSO to be heard to the best advantage. Audience response was excellent and critical reaction very favourable. Harry Rolnick of the *South China Morning Post* of 13 August said of the operatic concert:

> *'Both orchestra and singers were up to the task. Nobody could say the Irish played the opening Freischutz overture with Weber's fear and trembling intact. But those horns were faultless, the strings shivered appropriately".*

The nature of the tour and its programme was untypical and it showed the versatility of the NSO in a very wide ranging series of unusual events. As this excursion took place immediately prior to the Orchestra's annual holidays, many of

Albert Rosen

the musicians decided to trek further into the Orient and even the Southern Hemisphere before making circuitous journeys back to Ireland and the next series of home concerts. Twice since then, the NSO under Kasper de Roo has been overseas - once to the UK, in February 1997 with Barry Douglas as soloist, playing in Glasgow, Edinburgh and London's Royal Festival Hall, and once, with a concert on 5 May 1997 at the Innsbruck Saal Tirol Kongresshaus as part of that venue's international series of visiting orchestras.

Death of Albert Rosen

Albert Rosen had a number of concerts during 1996. On 19 January he partnered Marzio Conti in Carl Reinicke's Flute Concerto and, still keeping off the beaten track, Piers Lane was his soloist in Moritz Moszkowski's Piano Concerto on 13 December. Mr Rosen was back on the rostrum for the New Year's Eve concert which, due to an unprecedented demand, was repeated on the afternoon of New Year's Day. While Mr Rosen had been unwell during the course of 1996 he appeared to be his usual self during these concerts and he left for a series of engagements in Australia in early 1997.

Fate took matters in hand. Albert Rosen returned to Dublin in May to conduct the Last Night of the Bank of Ireland/RTÉ 'Proms' at the RDS. Not feeling well, he was admitted to St Vincent's Hospital and three days later, on 23 May, Albert Rosen, beloved by his musicians and his many, many admirers, lost his battle against the illness he bravely fought for some time. Over thirty years' service to music in Ireland had come to an end.

There was a memorial service in Dublin's Peppercanister Church at which members of the Orchestra played a musical tribute. Among a number of sincere eulogies was one from Brian O'Rourke, former principal clarinet of the NSO. I quote from part of it:

> *'He was concerned with the cultivation of all the orchestral virtues and it is said that, in his hands, the RTÉSO took on a mid-European identity. His main artistic purpose, however, was to capture the spirit of whatever music he was performing. He was a genuine romantic, a throwback to the late 19th century and belonged to an age before recording made musical interpretation acceptable only within very narrow confines.*
>
> *It is impossible to speak of Albert without thinking of opera. He was a creature of the theatre and his opera performances at the Wexford Festival are legendary; the white heat of* Katá Kabanová, *the frenzy of* The Gambler, *the malevolence of* The Turn of the Screw *or the comedy of* The Devil and Kate.
>
> *Because of his propensity to spring into the air at dramatic moments, the musicians of the RTÉ orchestras referred to him as the Bouncing Czech. However, in recent years he was affectionately known as Big Al; he was truly a big man and a big musician and, in the opinion of many, he had greatness in him'.*

Charles Acton writing about Albert Rosen commented:

> *'It was to all our great joy, in the chaotic days following Tibor Paul's departure, that RTÉ's head of Music,*

Gerard Victory, appointed Albert as principal conductor of the RTÉ Symphony Orchestra....Our orchestra (and we) needed a conductor who would train this fine band of musicians and make it into a good coherent body, which would sound with one unified, disciplined, warm-hearted voice, with its own collective personality, in any sort of music under any sort of visiting conductor. That was what Albert did.

At its beginning Jean Martinon made it a good orchestra. Tibor Paul made it an orchestra that our often philistine leaders recognised as a national asset that could not be ignored - and gave it a pride in its own self. Albert gave it and its individual members a warm-hearted personality which it never lost'.

In an obituary in *The Irish Times*, Richard Pine wrote:

'He personified the meeting point of west and east that lies along the axis of Vienna-Prague, the cities in which he was born and bred...

He would always speak of the music (as he did of everything else) in a down-to-earth, unpretentious way which nevertheless got to the heart of the matter - the point where you were connected to what made the music live.

It was this utter musicianship and musicality that made him the fine and great personality who illuminated everyone who came in contact with him...

Nowhere was this more evident than in the orchestra pit of the opera house, where Rosen was king. His command of every phrase, every gesture, every nuance, brought shapely dynamism to the genre of music-theatre...

The European tours which he conducted in 1976 and 1980...marked the beginning of the NSO's international reputation. Between Rosen and a later Principal, Bryden Thomson, lies the chief credit for the creation of the NSO as a firmly-based international ensemble...

Age did not diminish his vigour or his style, but it did increase his stature as he visibly matured, growing confident and accustomed to a life that had not earned him the top international laurels but had brought him acclaim and an enviable, reputation among his peers'.

On 28 September the NSO presented a Tribute to Albert Rosen at the NCH with a programme of Smetana, Dvořák and Janáček. It was conducted by Oliver von Dohnanyi, Music Director of the National Theatre in Prague, where Albert Rosen had conducted for many years. Proceeds from the concert went to the Irish Cancer Society and the programme book contained a number of appreciations of the former Conductor Laureate. I give an extract from one by Bob Collins, Director-General, RTÉ:

'Albert Rosen was one of the most outstanding musicians to work in Ireland....It is difficult to believe that this robust and vigorous figure has been taken from us - far too early for someone who still had much to give and to garner from his life in music. A hard worker, a charming and sophisticated gentleman, and above all a superb musician, he will be sadly missed by all who had the privilege of being his colleagues. We in RTÉ will

Alexander Anissimov

long cherish the memory of a man who so unassumingly came amongst us as a maestro, and enriched our lives'.

Conclusion

As we draw to the end of this selected history, it is rewarding to note that the 1996/97 and 1997/98 series of public subscription concerts by the NSO continue the policy of introducing new works, with Fergus Johnston's Flute Concerto (Gareth Costello/Anissimov), Raymond Deane's 'Krespel's Concerto' (Alan Smale/Pearce), which has been recorded for the Marco Polo label, and a triple concerto by James Wilson, 'For Sarajevo', marking his seventy-fifth birthday.

1998 sees Kasper de Roo entering his final period as Principal Conductor. The announcement that Alexander Anissimov, who is already living in Dublin with his family, is to replace him from autumn 1998 was greeted with tremendous enthusiasm by the public, with whom Anissimov has already established himself as a firm favourite, as was that of Gerhard Markson's appointment as Principal Guest Conductor.

A final look at a recent (12 September 1997) orchestral roll-call shows Elaine Clark as Alan Smale's co-leader, with Clodagh Vedres as deputy and Timothy Kirwan as principal in the first violins. David McKenzie is section principal of the seconds, supported by Vanessa Caminiti. Adèle Govier and Cheremie Allum are in the front desk of the violas and Aisling Drury Byrne continues to lead the cello section. Dominic Dudley and Wolfgang Eulitz head up the double-basses. Keeping matters in the family are mother and daughter, Clodagh and Anita Vedres (violins); father and daughter Tom and Melanie Briggs (horn and violin); while David Clark (violin) is brother of co-leader, Elaine.

The clarinets list John Finucane as principal, having taken over from Brian O'Rourke when a neuro-muscular condition in his right hand unfortunately ended his playing career. Thomas Rainer is among the trombones still so capably led by Seán Cahill, while Francis Magee is currently the NSO's tuba. Richard O'Donnell leads the percussion unit.

The Concerts Manager is now Claire Meehan, and Brian Jack supports Bene McAteer in the library. Maureen Donohoe continues in her demanding role of Planning Coordinator, while Eleanor Collier assists Laurie Cearr in Public Relations. Jennifer Reynolds carries out the tasks of Orchestra Secretary. Principal flautist, William Dowdall, now also serves on the Board of the National Concert Hall.

It is perhaps fitting that the season sees a large number of works by Mahler (the first four symphonies, the sixth symphony and *'Des Knaben Wunderhorn'*, a key work in Mahler's musical development), as it was with such cycles that Principal Conductors and the Orchestra have made their mark.